CONTENTS

PREFACE 5

INTRODUCTION 6

CHAPTER 1
THE LANDLORDS AND THE HUNGRY GRASS 7

CHAPTER 2
THE SCHOOL IN THE WOODLANDS & EDDY DUFFY 19

CHAPTER 3
THE HAUNTED MANSION —
   THE ARRIVAL OF THE NUNS 31

CHAPTER 4
BERGIN AND McDERMOTT 47

CHAPTER 5
THE MEN AND WOMEN BEHIND THE HEROES
The Gander and the Black and Tan 57

CHAPTER 6
THE CIVIL WAR 65

CHAPTER 7 THE LEAN YEARS	69
CHAPTER 8 THE EMERGENCY IN LOUGHGLYNN	81
CHAPTER 9 A JOB FOR ALL SEASONS	98
CHAPTER 10 BURY ME DACINT	108
CHAPTER 11 ECHOES OF LOUGHGLYNN	114
CHAPTER 12 LOUGHGLYNN SCHOOL IN THE THIRTIES AND FORTIES	133
CHAPTER 13 THE ROAD TO BALLAGH TOWN	150
CHAPTER 14 THE FIRST TIME I THOUGHT ABOUT LEAVING	155
CHAPTER 15 THE CALL OF THE WILD SWANS – Loughglynn revisited	160
SONGS	163

PREFACE

Vera McDermott was born in Aughaderry Loughglynn, Co. Roscommon. She was educated at Loughglynn school, and St Joseph's Secondary School Ballaghaderreen. She emigrated to London in 1949 and worked at various posts from waitress to bank clerk. After this she began a degree course at Liverpool University and later gained a master's degree at the University of Manchester. She met and married her husband Kenneth Brookes at university in 1958. She taught in Catholic schools and became a Deputy Head Teacher. She has two sons, one a doctor and the other a lawyer. After taking early retirement she took a diploma in teaching English as a second language and has taught English in various countries including Poland and Russia. She travels widely, and her main interest lies in Irish folklore and culture. She is a member of Comhaltas Ceoltórí Eireann, and whilst teaching in Catholic schools she encouraged and promoted her pupil's interest in their Irish heritage. The family have a house on the lake shore of Loughglynn.

INTRODUCTION

Loughglynn is an ancient village going back to before Christianity began. It is associated with Gaelic and Norman lords namely, McDermott, Costello, Fitzgerald, O'Connor and O'Hara. The McDermotts traditionally were descended from Murrayach Mullaghan who reigned over Connaught in the seventh century. They owned a large territory in the west of Ireland known as 'MacDermott Country' until deprived of the greater part of their lands by the British confiscations which followed the Cromwellian and Williamite Wars.

Prior to this the tribes were always at war with one another. The remaining round tower of Castlegallon, part of the original castle on the west side of the lake, was said to have been owned by the MacDermott clans at one time. After being driven from their fortress on the rock of Lough Key, the MacDermotts settled at Coolavin on the shores of Lough Gara. The family managed to hold onto a small parcel of their ancestral land through the penal times, but the power of the great Connaught chieftains was broken and Lord Dillon of Loughglynn was undisputed lord of all 'the rolling plains and grand Demesnes'. In Loughglynn today, few remember Lord Dillon, but there are numerous O'Gara's. O'Connor's, O'Hara's, O'Flynn's and Jordans, which goes to show that mercifully nothing is forever. "Nil in aon rud act seal".

CHAPTER ONE

THE LANDLORDS AND THE HUNGRY GRASS

> A starving population, an absentee aristocracy, an alien church, and the weakest executive in the world. (Disraeli)

The village of Loughglynn has been enshrined in song and story from time immemorial. It is rich with historic associations, and is still closely connected with its past through the relics of history that surround it. The original village according to tradition stood much nearer the lake and the site was marked by two enormous ash trees which flourished in the centre of the street. The present village was separated from the Demesne of Viscount Dillon by a thick screen of plantations. Weld, describes the baronetcy thus:

> The south western part of the barony of Boyle, stretching from Frenchpark to the verge of the county, where it joins Mayo, contains some of the most extensive tracts of bog in Roscommon; and yet here surrounded by water, is situated the rich Demesne of Loughglynn with its lake and fine hanging woods, the seat of Viscount Dillon.

The mansion which is now the convent of the Franciscan Missionaries of Mary, is situated on the northern bank of the lake. On the southern side of the lake, the relics of the original castle can be seen in the shape of the remaining round tower. Tradition has it that it was a well fortified building, defended at each angle by a tower. The castle is said to have been founded by a Fitzgerald of Mayo, descended from a daughter of Hugh O'Connor, who styled himself "King of Connaught". Stones from the original castle were used to build the new mansion which was very grand and imposing, in the midst of scenic beauty. A writer of the time describes the scene:

> The lake is almost an Irish mile in length. The scenery which surrounds it is picturesque, it has smooth green lawns sloping down to the water's edge, intermingled with trees. There is a wooded island in the centre, which breaks the continuous view of the lake, and gives great variety to the lines.

The Dillon estate, according to Grose, was initially granted to William Taafe, who sold it to Lord Dillon. Sir Theobold Dillon, King of Costelloe Galeen in the County of Mayo, was created the first Viscount Dillon in March 1621-22. The Dillons remained in Loughglynn for three centuries, and were absentee landlords for more than a century before the "PURCHASE OF LAND IRELAND ACT" 1891.

By signing the Act of Union in 1800 Ireland's ascendancy landlords – Lord Dillon of Loughglynn among them, demanded in return protection from the British government. This protection was given by enacting new statutes giving the power to evict tenants in arrears and enabling them to halt sub-division and joint tenancies. It also encouraged the displacement of a non-Irish landed aristocracy to London which resulted in the deterioration of their estates at home, with disastrous consequences for their tenants. In 1824 a landlord summed up their callous attitudes by saying "What the devil do I care how they live as long as they come to work when I want them."

Lord Dillon of Loughglynn and his family, as we have seen, were absentees, although the vast estate brought them £22,000 annually in rent. In the year 1841 a census of Ireland stated that there were eight million people, about three million of whom lived at poverty level. Cottiers, landless labourers and evicted small-holders made up three quarters of the rural population who lived in wretched conditions, barely at subsistence level, "subject every year to the chances of absolute destitution". By the early 1840s they were existing entirely on potatoes. They depended on a potato called the "lumper", which was prolific but was susceptible to disease. They lived in one roomed mud floored cabins, without chimneys or windows, and cultivated a small potato patch. In 1841 almost half a million hovels dotted the Irish countryside, especially in the south and west. A writer of the time describes the destitution on the Dillon estate:

> The barony of Roscommon, . . . furnishes examples of the most abject misery whether the housing or the clothing of the lower classes be considered. The very old and the very young appear occasionally half-covered, and with such shreds and tatters, that it is marvellous how these things, which do not deserve the

The Courthouse where Dillons tenants had to go to pay the rent. The derelict Courthouse today.

name of garments, can be put off or put on . . . The worst cabins are found in the vicinity of bogs, whither the poorer classes are attracted. . . Everything around these hovels, until the potato shows its green leaves, appears dark.

Disaster struck with the blight between 1845 and through the early 1850s the potato crop which was practically the only food for most of the people failed. The blight which struck in 1845 was caused by a rare fungus known as phytophthora infestans which appeared suddenly and decimated the crop. The destruction spread terror through the countryside, the great destroyer which ravaged the countryside and made it into a vast graveyard, not only claimed the dead, but also the traditions, the dreams, the hopes, the homes and the very identity of a nation. The hunger had come over the land.

In 1847 Lord Dillon was absent. If the anglo-Irish landlords had stayed on their estates, they would have seen at first hand the awful plight of their tenants, but most of the absentees had delegated power to their agents who, with the help of middlemen, generally exploited the tenants unmercifully. Loughglynn was lucky to some extent. The landlord's agent at Loughglynn was a Mr Charles Strickland who, though dour and humourless, was by all accounts a just man, and had a genuine feeling for the interests of his tenants.

STRICKLAND AND THE HUNGRY GRASS FIELD

Around the firesides in Loughglynn 'the Seanachies' passed down the horror stories of the black '47 in awed whispers. They maintained that the hunger that stalked the land with the famine could still be felt in the grass. Across the years I can still see 'ould Patric' with his gnarled hands clutching his ash-plant, and pointing it to 'the hungry field'. "Do ye see that field beyant? Ye can still detect the track of the ridges and furrows in it when the blight hit the pratie crop in black '47. No wan has ever grown a crop there since, or niver will again. Look at all the poisonous weeds and rank grass that's growin' there today, it's called "the hungry grass" an' if ye run or walk through it today ye'll feel an awful hunger, even if ye've just had your dinner. If ye listen ye

'The Round Tower' was part of Castlegallon said to be originally owned by the McDermott clans.

can hear the little starvin' childer cryin', cryin' for food". As children we used to "dare" each other to race through "the hungry grass" field and got scorched to death with nettles, scratched with tangled briars and rough marram-like grass. The tall rank grass made a weird whispering sound in the breeze, like a moaning mournful keen. We ran because we were scared that the ghosts of the tortured famine children were still there begging for food. "That field belonged to a man by the name o' Barney Clary", said Patric, "he lived in a cabin there with his wife Maggie, his son who had just got married, an' his new daughter in law. The ould couple used to sleep in 'the hag'. They gave up 'the high room' when their son Jamie got wed. Every morning ould Bart used to hobble down to the pratie field to see how the crop was doin'. The blight hadn't hit Loughglynn yet, but there were rumours that it had hit the mountainy country in the far west. Any road", said Patric, "wan morning in July the ould couple were wakened by the whining of their dog Ceilidh. What's wrong with that ould divil, said Bart, he's never cried before. Maggie crossed herself - it's the sign of a funeral, she muttered, but what's that awful stink? She held her nose. There's something bad up, said the old man. I heard them talking at the fair in Ballagh about the blight over in the mountains. You an' your ould blight, said Maggie, it's blight, blight, blight with ye all the time, ye're ravin' man, I've never seen a better field o' stalks than we have this year. Hould your whisht woman, said Barney, as he dragged his homespun trousers and his bawneen on, and hobbled down to the spud patch. The dog kept whining - God blast ye to Hell, said Barney, as a foul fog crept in from the west. ye couldn't see a hand in front o' you be all accounts, said Patric. The cryin' dog, the awful stink an' the thick fog frightened Maggie. The Cross o' Christ about me, she said as she snatched her rosary beads from the chimney piece and ran after Barney in her red tattered flannel petticoat and bare feet. When they got to the pratie patch it was an awful scene" said Patric, "all the neighbours were there wringing their hands an' crying, it's the blight, the hunger is on us, what's to become o' us. The men in threadbare bawneens with straw ropes tied around their homespun trousers were looking over the ditches at the blackened stricken crop. "Begob, only yesterday it was the best crop o' spuds ye ever saw" said an incredulous neighbour. "The praties might be alright in the ground", they said, it might only be the stalks that's damaged. They scrambled over the ditch said Patric an' desperately tried to break the blackened withered stalks, thinking this might save the spuds, but the stalks broke off in their hands and crumbled to dust. The tiny potatoes underneath were red rotten, a putrid slimy mess. Hunger was staring them in the face", said Patric. "The women were all cryin' and the childer were crowding round them asking for food. "What'll we do about the rints an' the lases?", said Long Mike a tall strapping giant of a man. "What are we goin' to ate, niver mind the rints", said Tom Dunne. "We'll all die with the hunger. It'll be worse if we're evicted", said Mike, "we'll die in the ditch with ne'er a shelter. Let's all go to see Strickland an' put our case before him. He might help an' he might not, there's wan thing for sure, he'll listen to us. Aye, he's a fair class o' a man, even if his face would crack in two if he smiled. Niver mind that, he can be alright if you're right with him. Be all accounts", said Patric, "it was heartbreakin' to hear the little childer cryin, so the women made a fire an' roasted the few 'poreens' that weren't rotten for a meagre meal.

The men set off an' half-way to the big house, they met Charles Strickland riding towards them on horseback. He was the colour o' death as he bade them 'good mornin'. I know it's not that good", he said as the men crowded around him all babbling together. "Not wan spud left, your honour, they're all as rotten as muck, that manes no money for the rint and no money for the lase, ye'r honour". Patric said Strickland raised his whip an' said, "calm down will ye, there'll be no rints charged an' no evictions on this estate until such time as things get getter. Ah, but what'll Lord Dillon say to this, savin' ye'r presence yeer only his agent, an' he's never here. I'm in charge here", said Strickland, "Lord Dillon will listen to me. Go back home, go back and I'll see what I can do for you. I promise you, I won't let any of you starve". Them were his very words be all accounts", said Patric. "God bless ye, ye'r honour, you've done a lot for us already by stoppin' the rints, at laste we'll have a roof over our heads". Strickland was as good as his word. he bought tons o' Injun male an' set up food depots all over the estate. His wife Maria an' his family worked day an' night to keep the poor fed. The big famine iron pots could be seen at Loughglynn house until the Dillons left. Strickland worked on all the relief committees, and wrote to the Lord Lieutenant of Ireland, begging him to sanction proposed public works, which would give employment to the people. Some of the roads led to nowhere, like the wan across the bog above, but they gave desperate people work an' saved them from starving. The famine fever was ragin. It was brought in by the homeless wretched people who wandered into the village looking for food and shelter. It was like a burial march", said Patric. "A lot o' the people came from Strokestown beyant – Major Denis Mahon's estate. He ordered a big clearance of the estate, thousands were evicted, an' the rest were given their passage money to Canada on 'the coffin ships'. He wanted the land for rarin' cattle an' sheep he could make more money on them you understand than the people. It was awful to see them dyin' in their thousands, in the ditches by the roadside huddled together. They looked like ragged skeletons, barely able to walk, all barefooted an covered in rags. They claimed it was much worse around Strokestown than here in Loughglynn. All you could see there they said was corpses heaped in ditches an' the death carts rattling along, carrying them to mass graves. Ye won't believe this", said Patric, "but they were followed by 'the crow-bar brigade', 'the house wreckers' an the military, they were awful times. Mahon was murdered at Doorty on his way home from Roscommon town — 'May the hearthstone of Hell be his bed-rest for ever', that's what the people said. 'Amen' said the awed listeners around our fire in Anghaderry.

When the hunger began to die down an' the praties began to grow again, Strickland met the tenants. At least half the people had gone. Strickland said this disaster was caused by a number of things, wan o' them was gross neglect by the landlord; the other was ignorance. "From now on I want my tenants to have a school and get some learnin'". "Arrah, haven't we the hedge schools, your honour, and the wan in the farmyard above, sure we're alright fur eddication. Ye'll all have seen the field beyant on the edge of the estate", said Strickland, "it's marked off for building on. That's going to be your new school for your childer so they can be educated. It'll also provide work for ye all to get ye back on ye'r feet. It's goin' to be the best school in Ireland with the best teachers. That's the story of the school yee'r in today, an' if it could talk it would tell a great yarn. Why did ould Strickland build a school at all, we kids grumbled as we realised we hadn't done our homework because ould Patric had mesmerised us with tales of the famine. We'd be in awful trouble tomorrow – an' it was no use tellin' our teacher that the dead famine children were still haunting the hungry grass field. No excuse for not learning our 6 times tables.

Loughglynn Town

Contains by Modern Survey 34 Acres

Dillon

No	Occupiers Names		No of Acres			Quality of Ground	Rate for Acre	Sums payable to Rector for annum		
			a	r	p		d	£	s	d
1	John	Rodgers	1	0	0	1st	10½		10	10½
2	Jas	Green	1	0	0	do	do		10	10½
3	Michl	Rodgers	1	0	0	do	do		10	10½
4	Pat	Smith	"	2	0	do	do		5	5¼
5	Elizabeth	Mongan	"	2	0	do	do		5	5¼
6	John	Caruby	"	2	0	do	do		5	5¼
7	Michl	Mulrooney	"	2	0	do	do		5	5¼
8	Pat	Donnellan	1	0	0	do	do		10	10½
9	W. Jas	Foly	2	0	0	do	do	1	8	1	9½
10	John	Mongan	"	2	0	do	do		5	5¼
11	John	Walls	"	2	0	do	do		5	5¼
12	Frans	McGuire	1	0	0	do	do		10	10½
13	Thos	McKelly Junr	1	0	0	do	do		10	10½
14	Pat	Connelly	1	0	0	do	do		10	10½
15	Pat	Quinn	1	0	0	do	do		10	10½
16	Chas	McDermot	1	0	0	do	do		10	10½
17	John	Hunt	1	0	0	do	do		10	10½
18	Anne	Cosgrave	4	2	0	2d	8½	2	11½	3	2½
19	Michl	McKelly	1	0	0	1st	10½		10	10½
20	W. R.	McGuire	1	0	0	do	do		10	10½
21	W. J.	McGuire	1	0	0	do	do		10	10½
22	Thos	McKelly Senr	3	0	0	do	do	2	5¾	2	8½
23	M. John	McKelly	1	0	0	do	do		10	10½
24	Jas	King	1	0	0	do	do		10	10½
25	Jas	Godow	1	0	0	do	do		10	10½
26	Maggy	Duffy	"	2	0	do	do		5	5¼
27	John	Plot	1	0	0	do	do		10	10½
28	W. Michl	Phillips	1	2	0	do	do	1	3	1	4½
29	M. John	Timothy	2	2	0	2d	8½	1	7¾	1	9½
			34	0	0			1	9	4

Joseph Sampson)
Arthur Browne) *Commissioners* £ 1 . 7 . 1

Signed

Aughadirry & Moyne

Lord Dillon — Contains by Modern Survey 165. 0. 00

No.	Occupiers Names	No of Acres			Quality of Ground	Rate for Acre	Sum payable to Rector for Annum		
		a	r	p		s d	£	s	d
1	Andy Duffy & Pt.	21	0	00	1st	10½	.	18	4½
2	Denis Casey & Pat	23	0	00	do	do	1	0	7½
3	Roger McDermot 6/4	20	0	00	do	do	.	17	11
4	John Mullowney & Pt.	30	0	00	2nd	8½	1	1	3
5	Thos. O'Brien & Pat	38	0	34	do	do	1	7	1
6	Mr. Dr. O'Brien	12	0	00	3rd	7	.	7	0
7	Widow Shannon	2	0	00	do	do	.	1	2
8	J. E. Strickland Esqr.	18	3	06	5	3	.	4	1½
		165	0	0		5	18	6½

Signed Joseph Snead
         Arthur Brown } Commissioners

Meelick

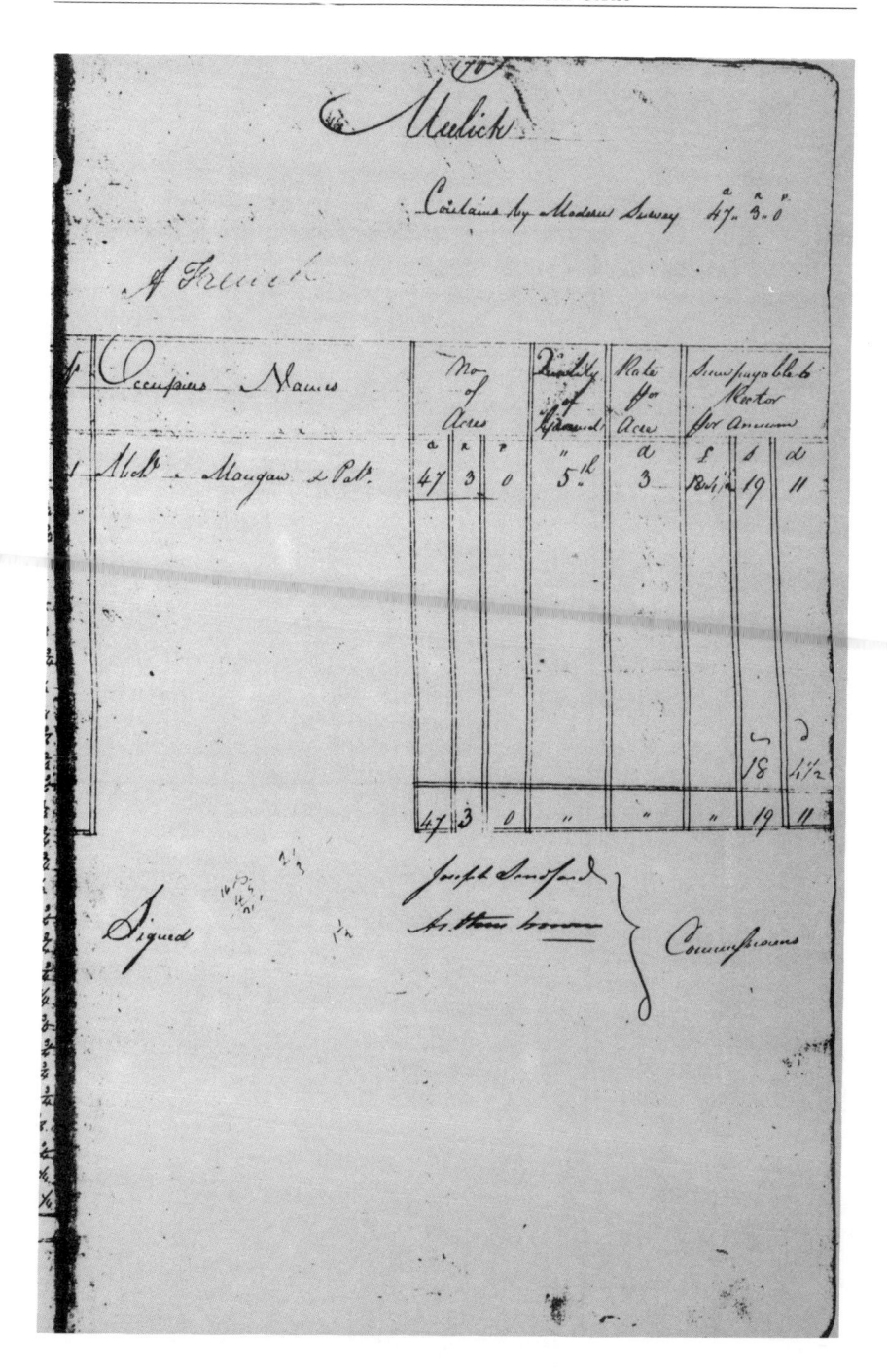

Contains by Modern Survey 47. 3. 0

A French

Occupiers Names	No. of Acres			Quality of Ground	Rate for Acre	Sum payable to Rector per Annum		
	a	r	p		a	£	s	d
1 Abel — Mangan & Pat.	47	3	0	5th	3	Bal.	19	11
							18	4½
	47	3	0	"	"	"	19	11

Signed

Joseph Sandford
Arthur Brown
} Commissioners

Lughadristin

Contains by Modern Survey 147.1.0

№	Occupiers Names	No of Acres	Quality of Ground	Rate for Acre	Sum payable to Rector for Acre	
1	Mr. Thos. Dillon	53.0.00	Third	7d	1.1	8.10.6¼
2	Darby Dolan	49.0.00	2nd	8½	1.1	17.14.8½
3	Mr. Denis O'Brien	30.0.00	3"	7	.	17.6
4	Dond. Gillan	3.0.00	4	5	.	1.1.3
5	James Rabbit	5.0.00	do	do	"	2.1
6	Mick Rabbit	5.0.00	do	do	"	2.1
7	Wm. Tapsey	2.1.00	do	do	.	11½
		147.1.0	"		4	9.15

Signed

Commissioners

2.16.9
1.13.0
3.9.2½

CHAPTER TWO

THE SCHOOL IN THE WOODLANDS AND EDDIE DUFFY

In an old school there is always listening and more is heard than spoken. The old school in Loughglynn stands there today proudly defying the ravages of time. It was built in 1850 on the periphery of the Dillon estate, mainly through the instigation of Charles Strickland who administered the estate in the absence of Lord Dillon, and was the first manager of the school. At this time there were no other schools in the district, except a haphazard system of education known as hedge schools, or pay schools. These schools lingered on until well after the great famine. My Mayo grandparents both attended a hedge school which was conducted in a cow-house. The teacher was an ex-student of the priesthood and they paid him 2d per week for tuition. Tradition has it that the school in Loughglynn which preceded the new school was housed in the farmyard in the shadow of the round tower which was the only tower left of the original Castle – Castle Gallagh which initially had four towers. The remaining tower was originally used for a garrison of soldiers who, it is said, were brought there by Strickland around about 1817 in order to defend himself and the people from attacks by an organ-

Loughglynn old School today.

ised group who called themselves 'Ribbon-men'. The militia were transferred to a barrack on the estate and the round tower was subsequently used to house prisoners awaiting trial and was referred to as 'the black hole', or dungeons. As children we used to climb the spiral stone steps to the top of the tower where we were rewarded by a magnificent view which encompassed Charlestown and the Sligo mountains. It was in this historic environment where Loughglynn children received their education prior to the building of the new school in 1850. The school was opened on February 11th 1856, there were no other schools in the district, (the aforementioned pay school seemingly was not regarded as such). The new school was built of stone and mortar and was 107 ft high, its length was 317 ft and its breadth 197 ft. In a report upon application by Mr Charles Strickland for, and towards the payment of teachers' salaries and a supply of books, the following information was given. The village of Loughglynn was about a quarter of a mile off with about 700 inhabitants. "It contained about 44 cabins, and four houses of two stories, the houses had the appearance of being comfortable". It also had a

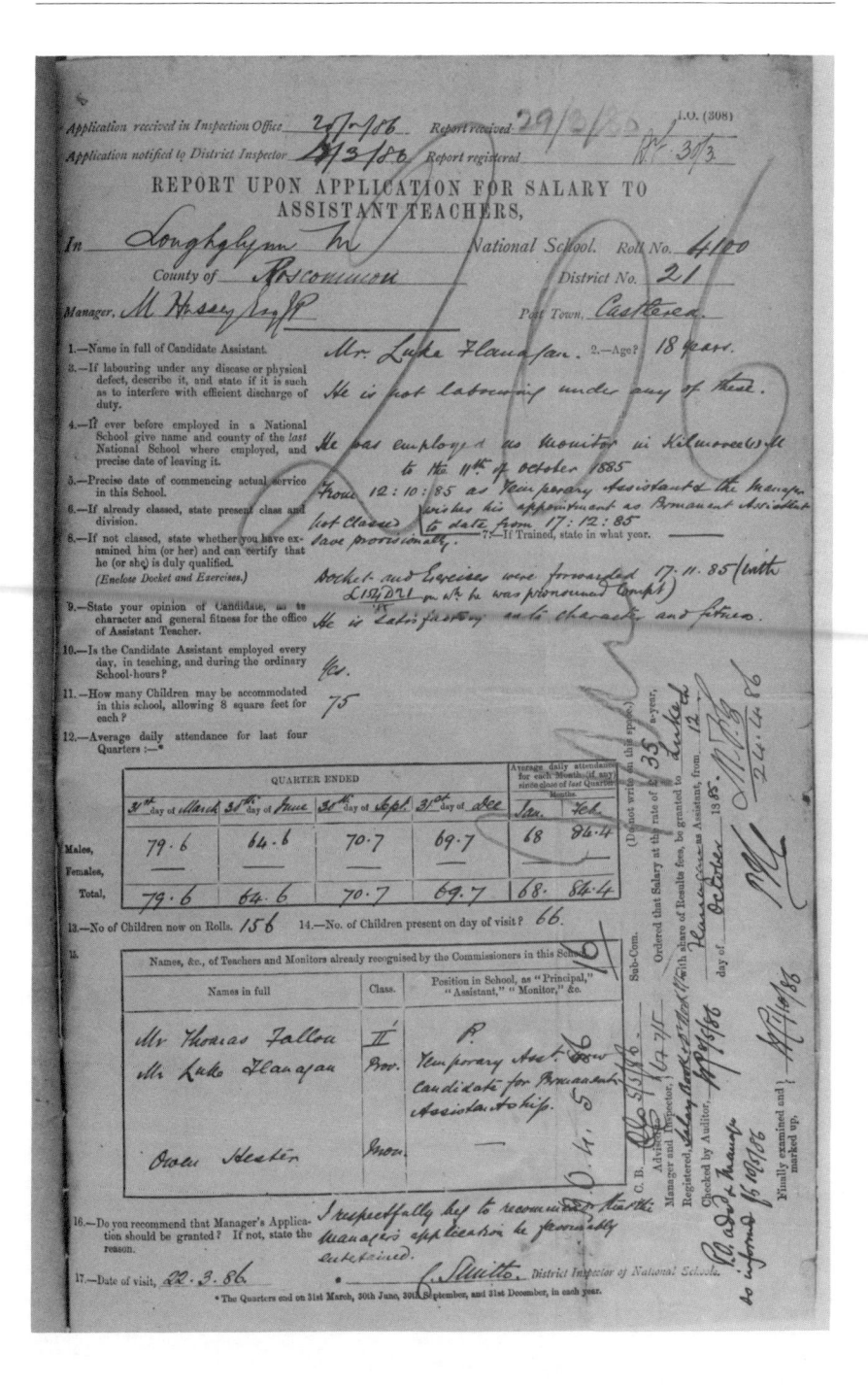

REPORT UPON APPLICATION FOR SALARY TO ASSISTANT TEACHERS,

In _Loughglynn_ National School. Roll No. _4100_
County of _Roscommon_ District No. _21_
Manager, _M Hussey_ Post Town, _Castlerea_

1. —Name in full of Candidate Assistant. — *Mr. Luke Flanagan.* 2.—Age? *18 years.*
3. —If labouring under any disease or physical defect, describe it, and state if it is such as to interfere with efficient discharge of duty. — *He is not labouring under any of these.*
4. —If ever before employed in a National School give name and county of the last National School where employed, and precise date of leaving it. — *He was employed as Monitor in Kilmorecs N.S. to the 11th of October 1885*
5. —Precise date of commencing actual service in this School. — *From 12:10:85 as Temporary Assistant & the Manager*
6. —If already classed, state present class and division. — *Not Classed wishes his appointment as Permanent Assistant to date from 17:12:85*
8. —If not classed, state whether you have examined him (or her) and can certify that he (or she) is duly qualified. (Enclose Docket and Exercises.) — *Have provisionally. 7.—If Trained, state in what year. — Docket and Exercises were forwarded 17.11.85 with L13/D21 on wh. he was pronounced Compt.*
9. —State your opinion of Candidate, as to character and general fitness for the office of Assistant Teacher. — *He is satisfactory as to character and fitness.*
10. —Is the Candidate Assistant employed every day, in teaching, and during the ordinary School-hours? — *Yes.*
11. —How many Children may be accommodated in this school, allowing 8 square feet for each? — *75*
12. —Average daily attendance for last four Quarters:—

	31st day of March	30th day of June	30th day of Sept.	31st day of Dec	Jan.	Feb.
Males,	79.6	64.6	70.7	69.7	68	84.4
Females,						
Total,	79.6	64.6	70.7	69.7	68	84.4

13.—No of Children now on Rolls. *156* 14.—No. of Children present on day of visit? *66*

15.

Names in full	Class.	Position in School, as "Principal," "Assistant," "Monitor," &c.
Mr Thomas Fallon	II	P.
Mr Luke Flanagan	Prov.	Temporary Asst now Candidate for Permanent Assistantship
Owen Hester	Mon.	—

16.—Do you recommend that Manager's Application should be granted? If not, state the reason. — *I respectfully beg to recommend that the Manager's application be favorably entertained.*

17.—Date of visit, *22.3.86* _C. Smith_ District Inspector of National Schools.

A. 90.

No. of Letter requesting Aid __13195-85__
Received in Office __3/m/85__
Form of Application Despatched __10/n/85__
Returned to Office __21/n/86__
Acknowledged by Circular __25/3/86__
Notified to Inspector _____
Report Received __30/3/86__
Application Referred to Sub-Committee __31/3/86__

Ent'd in App. Book

I.O. (307)

QUERIES

TO BE ANSWERED ON APPLICATION TO THE COMMISSIONERS OF NATIONAL EDUCATION FOR AID TOWARDS THE

SALARY OF AN ASSISTANT TEACHER

IN _Loughglynn_ NATIONAL SCHOOL, Roll No. _4100_

District No. _94_ County of _Roscommon_

1.—State the Christian and Surname of the Candidate Assistant. } _Luke Hanafan_

2.—State also the Age, and furnish evidence of Age and Health if candidate was never recognized as National Teacher (i.e. Principal or Assistant) before. } _18½ years._
(See enclosed instructions)

3.—If the Candidate ever taught in any other National School, state the name and county of such National School, and date of leaving it. } _Served as Monitor in Kilmovee M. Nat. School No.1, County Mayo for three years up to his appointment in this School._

4.—State the precise date on which the Candidate Assistant commenced to give actual service in this School. } _12th October 1885_

5.—Is the Candidate Assistant employed in teaching every day, and during the whole of the ordinary School hours? } _Yes._

M. Hopson Manager or Correspondent
_19_ day of _Feby 86_
Ballea Post Town.

dispensary and a Catholic chapel. The Protestant parish church was situated at some distance in the west of the village. The village skirting the public road on one side was separated from the Demesne by a thick screen of plantations. The school was established in 1856, the townland was Loughglynn in the parish of Tibohine and the barony of Frenchpark. It consisted of four rooms, one of which was used as a school-room. Three windows slid up and down, the floor was boarded. Other rooms were intended for industrial education. There were seven desks and a book press with lock and key. There were no blackboards and no clock. There was no bell and no canes. There were strict rules laid down about corporal punishment; it was discouraged and could only be exercised in extreme cases of delinquent behaviour, if at all.

> It shall be the duty of every teacher in this school to instil in their pupils, loyalty and respect for their sovereign – Her gracious majesty Queen Victoria.

This logo was displayed in a prominent place in the school room. Strickland's application was received on February 8th 1856 and an inspection was arranged for the 28th day of December 1856. Mr Strickland sanctioned the appointment of Miss Ann Duffy the first principal teacher in the school with her sister as assistant. Ann Duffy was educated and 'received instructions in the order of teaching' in the Commissioners and Model Schools, Marlborough Street, Dublin. When asked about her testimonials and her fitness for office, Mr Charles Strickland stated that he knew Miss Duffy personally and also as a professional woman, she taught in Swinford and in Kilmovee and was of excellent character. The Duffy family came to Loughglynn in February 1856 from their native town of Ballaghadereen. The family consisted of a mother, sister and two young brothers, one of whom Eddie was destined to become a Fenian leader. Mr Strickland had a residence built for them very close to the school. It was built in the style of the other houses in the neighbourhood and had a thatched roof and three to four rooms. It was situated on the periphery of Lord Dillon's demesne in the midst of stunning scenic beauty. The avenues of trees leading to the stately mansion were like vast cathedral domes as they met overhead to form an arch. The lake which according to tradition was once a race-course but was made into a lake at the instigation of the 8th Viscount Dillon as a birthday surprise for his wife, had a picturesque wooded island in the centre, and green lawns sloping down to its shores where the trees stooped down to kiss the lapping water. As well as being thickly wooded, the demesne contained many areas of fertile grazing land where the agents' cattle roamed. The estate was protected by a 6 ft wall which was constructed by Dillon's tenantry at a mere pittance of 1d a day when the Act of Union was passed in 1800. it was a way of employing men for miles around, who were reduced to poverty and idleness due to the continued part failure even then of the potato crop which foreshadowed the famine. It was said that bullocks' and people's blood was used to reinforce the mortar. Outside the walls were the poor homes of the tenants, some very small land holders and cottiers. This was the background to Eddie Duffy's youth, and must have inspired him with patriotism and zeal for betterment. He witnessed the evils of landlordism at a very close range.

The terrible experiences of the famine left many Irish people determined never to allow the same circumstances to happen again. In 1856 James Stephens, a former civil engineer, returned to Ireland from Paris where he had mixed with revolutionaries and fought at the barricades in 1851. He toured the country to assess people's opinions and the prospects for another uprising. Thomas Clarke Luby and Stephens founded a new secret organisation on St Patrick's Day 1858 in Dublin. They became known as the Irish Republican Brotherhood and aimed to make Ireland an independent republic by force of arms. The movement was strongest in the towns and the chief recruiting grounds were the trade unions and drapery establishments. Eddie Duffy was apprenticed to the drapery business at McDonaghs in Castlerea. He stayed there for three years, enjoyed his work and was very popular with both his employer and colleagues. When he left, Mrs McDonagh presented him with a prayer-book as a souvenir which was inscribed with her warmest wishes for a successful

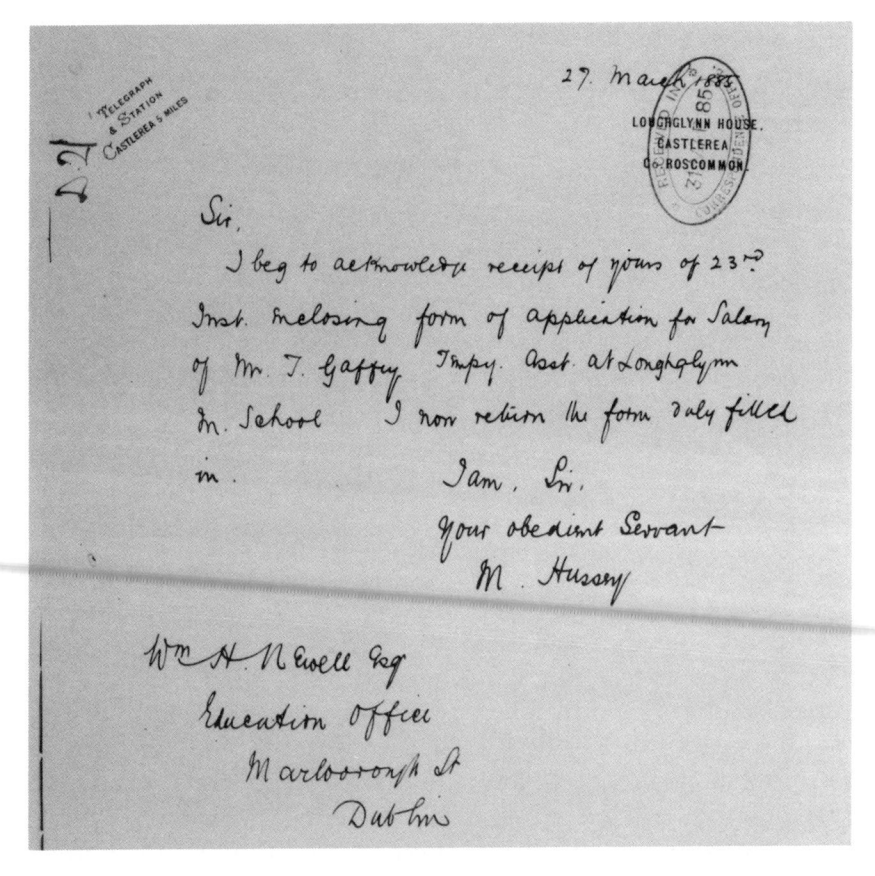

> 27 March 1885
> Loughglynn House,
> Castlerea,
> Co. Roscommon
>
> Sir,
>
> I beg to acknowledge receipt of yours of 23rd inst. enclosing form of application for Salary of Mr. J. Gaffey Impy. Asst. at Loughglynn Nl. School I now return the form duly filled in.
>
> I am, Sir,
> Your obedient Servant
> M. Hussey
>
> Wm. H. Newell Esq
> Education Office
> Marlborough St
> Dublin

future. This prayer book was his greatest treasure for the rest of his life. Whilst in Castlerea, he returned to Loughglynn every weekend, and heard Mass and prayed in the chapel near his home. He met his young friends and almost certainly talked about rebellion and revolution. He had become a committed Fenian. Revolution and rebellion was filling the air as they walked beside the shady demesne and dreamed of a free Ireland.

Eddie went to Dublin from Castlerea and there met the Fenian leaders, O'Donovan Rossa, Thomas Clarke Luby and John O'Leary. Eddie and Ellen O'Leary, John's sister, fell in love and became engaged to be married.

At this time the Fenians were feverishly preparing for a revolution. Their leader James Stephens had predicted with great

Memorial to Eddie Duffy on the site of his home in Loughglynn.

confidence that 1865 would be 'the year of action'. He procrastinated; things were not going according to plan - there were money and arms problems. Eddie Duffy was deputed to organise the west. Initially he travelled from place to place without exciting suspicion, but eventually he was arrested in his native town of Ballagh by the R.I.C. He was subsequently released as no incriminating evidence was found on him. From then on he had to move about with greater caution using various disguises. A republic was the objective of the Fenians and the doctrine which Duffy preached was republican. he never conceived the idea of a partitioned Ireland. Events began to move very quickly, the British government sensing revolution moved quickly to crush it. On 15th September a strong force of police arrested many of the Fenian leaders including John O'Leary, editor of The Irish People, a Fenian newspaper, Thomas Clarke Luby and Jeremiah O'Donovan Rossa. O'Leary and Luby were sentenced to 20 years each for treason while Rossa was sentenced to life. Early one morning the soldiers searching for James Stevens in a house outside Dublin where he was found, also discovered Eddie Duffy and other Fenian leaders, all of whom were arrested, tried and sentenced to varying terms of imprisonment in English prisons. Eddie Duffy was incarcerated in Millbank prison, where he and his fellow prisoners, one of whom was O'Donovan Rossa were exposed to insult, calumny and harsh treatment. They were chained in irons, given a diet of bread and water and placed in solitary confinement. Eddie probably contracted tuberculosis as a result of this harsh treatment.

The rising in '67 came and was a failure in as much as it failed to achieve its ends, but it inspired the Irish people and gave them new life and hope which was totally demoralised by the effects of the great famine. On a bleak January morning when gusts of snow and wind howled across the icy lake at Loughglynn and moaned eerily through the tall trees, the news that Eddie Duffy was dead in Millbank struck a note of infinite sadness and despair throughout the land, but nowhere as deep as in the cottage by the wood, for here was the grief of his mother, the brother and the sisters. O'Donovan Rossa captured the depths of this sadness in his poem about the death of Eddie Duffy.

> The mother's instinct tells her that her dearest boy is dead,
> That gifted mind, that noble soul from earth to Heaven has fled,
> As the girls rush towards the door
> And look upon the trees to catch that sorrow-laden wail that's borne on the breeze.

Neighbours and friends came and tried to console them and give them sympathy. The girls' positions in the school were in serious jeopardy, as no landlord in Ireland would be in favour of rebellion as obviously the landlord was the strongest link in the chain that bound Ireland to Britain.

Mr Charles Strickland therefore had no option but to terminate the employment of Ann Duffy and her sister as teachers in the school. They were in a powerful position to indoctrinate the children of his tenantry in seditions and revolutionary practices, so they were dismissed. Heartbroken, they tore themselves away from the cottage in the wood where O'Donovan Rossa, Kickham, O'Leary and Luby met and where many a council of war was held. Fenian women formed their own organisation, they collected funds for help and counsel for the prisoners and fed those who were sick. Ellen O'Leary, fiancee of Eddie Duffy, poetess and sister of John O'Leary frequently visited the cottage in the wood. She participated in the Fenian women's movement alongside Mrs Luby and Mary O'Donovan Rossa.

After a decade the Land League was launched in the country and it had strong support in Loughglynn because Eddie Duffy's young friends were now mature men and they were determined to carry on the fight, so they joined the land league. Tenant farmers in the west were faced with plummeting prices for their agricultural products. This disaster was compounded by two consecutive bad harvests. They were therefore unable to pay their rents to the landlords or their debts to the shopkeepers. Eviction stared them in the face. The shadow of the mass evictions of black '47 loomed ominously and they dreaded a repetition of the horrors of that desperate time. They began to organise mass meetings in 1897-98 to protest against rack renting and evicting landlords. They demanded the three Fs, fair rent, fixity of tenure, and freedom of sales. Michael Davitt, a native of Straide, Co. Mayo, whose family were evicted in 1850, and who now lived in Lancashire, visited his native Mayo in 1879, and saw the mounting distress of the people. He was a member of the Irish Republican brotherhood. In Mayo local activists, with the help of Davitt, organised a mass meeting at Irishtown, a village near the meeting point of Counties Galway, Mayo and Roscommon. The posters announced:

The West's awake –
"Great Tenant right meeting in Irishtown"

Several thousand people arrived for the meeting including a big contingent from Loughglynn. From the platform James Daly called for "the land of Ireland for the people of Ireland" and stated that "those who take the land of the evicted are the enemies of the country and are as culpable as the landlords". As a result of this meeting, landlords in Mayo, Galway and Roscommon quickly allowed rent reduction. Many tenants encouraged by Davitt and the land league made up their minds to 'hold the harvest', keeping enough to cover their needs and paying only the rent they could afford. This strategy was responsible for coining a new word in the English language, "Boycott". An agent in Mayo, Captain Boycott was so cruel to his tenants that men refused to work for him, shopkeepers refused to do business with him, he was totally ostracized. He had to import military and Orangemen from the North to gather in his crops. He was "boycotted". People who took the land of the evicted were contemptuously described as "land-grabbers". They were also boycotted. Fanny Parnell sister of Charles Stewart Parnell wrote a ballad called "Hold the Harvest". Davitt described it as 'the marsellaise of the Irish people. It was evocative of 'the great famine'.

> Three hundred years your crops have sprung
> by murdered corpses fed,
> Your butchered sires, your famished sires,
> for ghastly compost spread;
> Their bones have fertilised your fields,
> Their blood has fallen like rain,
> They died that you might eat and live,
> God, have they died in vain?

Charles Strickland knew that this time round the people were determined to regain their birthright. He retired without a struggle. He was as heartbroken as in his own way he loved Loughglynn. The school in the woodlands that Strickland started continued. In 1886 the boys' school was manned by Mr Thomas Fallon, Mr Luke Flanagan and Mr Owen Hester. The names of these teachers are still familiar in Loughglynn today. Thomas Fallon the principal teacher was evicted from his home in Aughaderry which was then a teachers' residence. The house is still there today. Like the Duffys before him, he and his family emigrated to America. During Charles Strickland's stewardship evictions were rare in Loughglynn. For a short period however, after he left, the son of a notorious Kerry landlord took over and attempted to put back the clock in order to strengthen the landlords' position and evictions again became common. The young friends of Eddie Duffy now old, saw one victory achieved. In 1891 the Purchase of Land Ireland Act was passed and in 1885 the Land Commission gave the tenants purchasing money which they guaranteed to repay. So after centuries of landlordism the Demesne lands were divided among the rightful owners - the dispossessed tenantry. Tradition has it that they tore down the ornate iron gates of oppression that led to the mansion; they lit tar barrel bonfires and danced and sang in the avenues and rydes that for centuries were the preserve of the Dillon landlords. Eddie Duffy who lived in the cottage by the wood and who died in a bleak unfriendly London prison to free Ireland from the curse of landlordism did not die in vain. The friends of Eddie Duffy's youth were now landowners. As the new century approached bringing with it a new era and more high drama, the school looked on and listened; the new teachers in charge were Mr McGetrick and Mrs O'Connor. The cottage in the wood was demolished, the magnificent trees which gazed down on the home of Eddie Duffy and which Rossa referred to so poignantly in his poem are no longer there. A monument to the memory of Eddie Duffy now stands on the spot where once the cottage stood, the cottage where Clarke, Luby, O'Leary and O'Donovan Rossa made history and where Eddie Duffy, one of Loughglynn's bravest and much loved sons lived and was waked by his family and friends. O'Donovan Rossa from his prison cell succinctly describes the scene.

> In the dead house you are lying
> and we'd wake you if we could,
> But they'll wake you in Loughglynn, Ned,
> In the cottage by the wood

CHAPTER THREE

THE HAUNTED MANSION – THE ARRIVAL OF THE NUNS 1900-1903

The new century heralded a more hopeful era for the people of Loughglynn and their school in the woodlands. The great estates were breaking up, the Dillon estate was purchased by the Congested District Board for £29,000 in 1899 and the Demesne lands were divided among the tenants. The rich demesne fields which were 'grace and favour' for the landlords' employees, for instance, stewards, herdsmen, important administrative clerks, were now owned by local farmers. The fields retained their former names and were steeped in history and local lore. Tipper fields, three fields bordering the avenue were named after a herdsman called Tipper. The Hope field also was named after a steward of Lord Dillon. The nursery was an area of land which was devoted to nurturing rare plants, shrubs, exotic flora and fauna from distant lands in the British Empire, visited by the Dillon family, many of whom worked and lived there in positions of authority both in army and civilian life. The nursery was the cherished preserve of the Strickland family. The most famous field is the 'White Horse' field. This semi-circular field is situated between two thickly wooded areas in the heart of the demesne, and is adjacent to the famous woodlands where the young freedom fighters died in 1921. Charles Strickland who was a close friend of the Prince of Wales, later King Edward VII, was presented with a magnificent white charger by the Prince. The horse was grazed in this field. At this time a famous band of German musicians wandered through the country. Like Carolan the blind music maker, they visited the big houses and entertained the gentry. They frequently visited the Dillon estate and played martial airs. When the horse heard these stirring tunes, he pranced around, harness jingling keeping time to the music as he had been trained in war. People, mainly gentry, came in their hundreds to see this amazing phenomenon. The White Horse field is and was associated with the ghosts of the gentry and is treated with great respect by the local people. An old man nicknamed Mr M'Friend who lived adjacent to the wood and the field, would under no circumstances go via that field to Driminagh bog where his turf bank was situated. "By jingo, I'm never going through that haunted field", he said. This field was used as a short-cut by the local people who had turf banks in Driminagh. Jamesy maintained that at certain times – very early morning, and bright moonlit nights, the charger could be heard prancing round the field breathing fire to a musical accompaniment. Across the years I can still see Jamesy with his ashplant and his home-made cart and black donkey, going all the way around the avenue and the circle to the bog in order to bypass the White Horse field. It was an exciting time for the local people, the freedom to be able to own and walk on the land of their fathers which was brutally wrenched from them by the planter oppressors and which until now they could only glimpse over the high demesne walls was a major achievement. The elegant mansion was now empty. There was no sound of revelry by night, the time had come when the music had to stop. After Charles Strickland departed, it was said that the big house became a centre of wild all night parties and jollification. When the third storey of the mansion was gutted by fire, one of the employees raced to the hall door to alert the agents Hussey and Jackson about the blaze. The motto of the landlords was "servants should not be seen and not be heard". The rules were strict, servants were admonished not to walk in the garden unless permitted, or unless they knew that all the family were absent. Stephen braved the lions in their den and banged furiously on the hall door. A flunkey answered it, reported it to the revellers who, unaware of the fire, promptly ordered Stephen off the doorstep in a most insulting and overbearing manner. The third storey was gutted and never restored. The administrative offices, or the court house, were turned into stables for the parish priest's cattle. As a child I remember sheltering there on my way to Loughglynn and even then the magnificent fireplace intrigued me. I used to run my fingers along the intricate mahogany mouldings and imagine what it must be like to work in these beautiful rooms. The windows I think were Georgian. The cattle looked on indifferently at their elegant quarters, and the rooms if they could talk must have been dismayed at their new occupants and their own fall from baronial grace. People from as far away as Ballyhaunis and Kiltullagh used to come with their rent to Loughglynn. They had of course to walk, and it's a long dreary way from Kiltullagh to Loughglynn, especially on cold winter nights when the lochans were flooded. My grandmother told me that the Ballyhaunis people referred to Mr Strickland as "Strick-the-land". He was reported to be a benevolent landlord's agent but he tended to treat the tenants as if they lacked judgment and intelligence. He could at times be quite harsh and ruthless with his tenants. A family in the Ballyhaunis area had a dispute with their neighbours about the trespassing of poultry on the little patch; the family who were called the O'Donnells and were allegedly responsible for the trespass, were stripped of their five acres by Strickland and given a half an acre to support themselves. Later when the land was divided the O'Donnells retained this half acre field, emigrated to America and set the field at one shilling a year to a neighbour. They never returned and that neighbour still retains the field. When the tenants came with their rents which were paid in gold sovereigns - after the money was counted it was thrown into a store trough of water to cleanse it for fear of contamination before it was sent to the landlord. My grandfather remembered a poor widow-woman, barefoot and in rags who walked from Tulrahan to pay part of her rent.

She was weak from cold and hunger. The sovereigns were thrown into the stone trough for the cleansing process before being sent to the landlord. The widow begged for time to pay the rest of the Autumn gale rent, but she was threatened with eviction if the remaining money wasn't forthcoming within a week. Dejectedly she set off on the return journey. She was found floating in the lochans on the road to Ballyhaunis; the lochans had burst their banks with the autumn floods and she was too weak to fight the swirling water and drowned.

So the big house and its inhabitants had a catalogue of skeletons in its elegant cupboards which boded ill for any new occupants that might want to live there. It was full of ghosts. The story tellers were in their element around the blazing turf fires on winter nights. The Seanachies told hair raising tales of the exploits and cruelty of the landlords and their agents down through the centuries. Legend had it that a bygone wicked agent was abducted by a group of desperate tenants who were evicted from their cabins just before the Christmas season. It was a particularly harsh winter and one of the young evicted women gave birth to her baby in a ditch near the tumbled cabin. Both the mother and baby died. The young father vowed, as he held his dead wife, that he would get his revenge. He said "I promise you Katie before God, that before next year is out, the devil who did this to you will meet his brother in hell". The rest of the family and neighbours cursed the agent, not loud but deep. "May the hearthstone of Hell be his bed-rest for ever" they said. The young man kept his promise, he took to the hills and with help from servants inside the big house, he and his dispossessed friends stormed into the magnificent drawing room overlooking the dark lake. The agent had his feet on the fender and was enjoying a hot toddy before a blazing fire. Before he had time to open his mouth to summon help he was dragged into an anteroom off the main hall and shot with a rusty pistol. It was said that the room where he was murdered was sealed off because his ghost appeared there every night at the same time that the murder was committed. The perpetrators were arrested and imprisoned in the black hole of the remaining round tower. They were tried in the local court house and sentenced to death by hanging in public as an example to anyone else who attempted to molest or injure or murder the landlords or their agents.

Another gripping story was 'the headless rider'. At midnight he was, according to legend frequently seen riding round the circle on a coal black charger. Both rider and horse disappeared in a cloud of mist if approached. The favourite story was the one about the viscount's daughter who fell in love with a tenant's handsome son whom she met on her morning carriage rides. She was very beautiful. He beguiled her with tales of his dispossessed ancestors who he said were chiefs in their own right. They were driven off their estates by Cromwellian planters and took to the hills. Later they were reinstated as tenants. He maintained that each generation in his family made wills leaving their former estates to their families. They always hoped they would regain their possessions and wealth. The young couple planned to elope to America, but the aristocratic beauty was betrayed by her maid and her handsome lover was arrested and deported to penal servitude for life on Van Diemens land. His family were evicted as a reprisal. It is said that the viscount's daughter pined for her lost love, went into 'a decline' and died of a broken heart. Legend had it that keening and sighing could be heard before the dawn at "the black stick" which was the trysting place for the lovers. The light which could frequently be seen in Sabbath Wood was another famous ghost lore. As a child I saw these lights myself; they turned out to be a phosphorescent property on the barks of some trees, and on very dark nights they emitted sharp glinting beams of light. The story tellers would have none of it; there was no scientific explanation, they were ghosts for sure, mostly the landlords and their agents escaping from hell - burning hell, the hell of the damned. "May the hearthstone of hell be their bed rest for ever".

THE DAY THE NUNS CAME

When the news broke that the big house was going to be used as a convent for a foreign missionary order of nuns called 'The Franciscan Missionaries of Mary', the local community were very surprised and very curious. "They're goin' to change it from sinners to saints", said the people, "but will they be able to live

Loughglynn House once the home of Lord Dillon now a Convent of the Franciscan Missionaries of Mary.

there with the ghosts, especially as the ghosts were evil. "They'll never get rid o' them, the whole place is haunted", was the general opinion. Nevertheless the nuns, a Belgian order of foreign missionaries, came to Loughglynn in 1903 at the request of Bishop Clancy, Bishop of Elphin who bought the mansion from the congested district board. My late father, Roger McDermott, was asked by the parish priest to meet the Reverend Mother and her assistant at the station in Castlerea. The conveyance that he had was an outside car, or jaunting car. In the centre it had a deep well for carrying goods. The two nuns had a straw mattress and a few small stools to start off their new convent. They appeared to be very poor; they were anxious to know if the previous owners had left any sticks of furniture which they could utilise. The Reverend Mother spoke English with a foreign accent. The mansion was cold and uninviting, the wind from the lake whistled and roared down the vast chimneys, the bare boards re-echoed to the sound of the sisters' shoes, which were a Dutch clog variety. My father made a roaring fire and boiled a kettle of water to make a hot drink of cocoa for the nuns. The high ceilings in the cavernous mansion, the elegant bare echoing staircase, with only flickering candle light to relieve the gloom made an ominous start for the fledgling convent. Soon the sisters were joined by other members of the Community, all of whom had specialised in various professions and skills. Their main work was spreading the gospel in countries which spanned the globe including 'the white man's grave', Liberia. For years in the entrance hall at Loughglynn Convent, there was a map of the world which pin-pointed all the convents in which their order worked. The local people naturally were intrigued with their new neighbours. The Order was strict and enclosed. However the nuns occasionally walked out in pairs for recreation purposes. Many of them were from the continent of Europe and spoke in their own tongue; they all wore the beautiful cream habit of St Francis. They were a direct contrast to their predecessors, who were arrogant and disdainful. The nuns were gentle and unobtrusive and were a favourite topic of conversation and speculation in the "rambling" houses. A favourite question was "Why do ye think good lookin' girls like them would join a convent?" An old fella shook his head wisely and said, "I'll give ye a written guarantee that they're disappointed lovers". "What I think",

said another wag, "is that they had no 'fortune' an they didn't want to be 'ould maids' so they 'joined up'." "I see what you mane, they wanted to have decent writin' on their tombstones, no wan wants to have 'Miss' plastered on their gravestone - would they?" "Well you're wrong about the fortune" said a young fella who spent a short time in a monastery. "They have to pop the money out to the Reverend Mother before she lets them put a foot inside the door". "Well, is that so", said the unbelieving listeners. "Mebbe they get paid for the job", said Jamesey. "Indade they don't, it's all done for 'the man above'. They're married to him you know" said Mary Jane. Married or not, Jamesy who believed in earning an honest bob was amazed. It's a very bad *do* if there's no "brass" in it at all (he was a seasonal worker in Yorkshire and picked up the local dialect). "How are they goin' to manage the ghosts?" That was another big question – ah, the holy wather'll get rid o' them, tis said most of the rooms are haunted. "Did ye hear the latest", said Ould Biddy. "I believe the Reverend Mother had an awful shock the other night, she heard a sharp ring on the hall door bell. When she opened the door a tall gentleman in a top hat greeted her. As he stepped forward she noticed that he had cloven feet. Frightened out of her life she seized an umbrella from the hall stand and dipped it smartly in the holy water fount and made a circle round her visitor who immediately disappeared in flames of fire. That'll be the ould agent who evicted families in three villages up the country, so that he could plant a wood for the shoot". "That's very true" said Tom Kilcourse. "I often heard me grandfather spake about him. From that day he never had a minute's luck and one windy night he hanged himself in the saddle room. Part of the rope that he used can be seen dangling there to this very day. Divil mend him!" "If you ask me", said a young fella, "there's more ghosts there than nuns. The best way to get shut o' the varmints is to get the Canon to bless the lake and pour the water over the whole damn lot, that'd soon shift them. If they did that they'd set fire to the bloody place, there's so many o' them, they'd go up in flames". "Well the Reverend Mother should bring a priest in to 'exercise' them or whatever they do". "A priest did ye say? No man not even the Pope himself is allowed to put his foot in the place - they're married to 'the man above' you know. The other day when they were out walkin' the council men were mending the road - there was a big hole in the middle. One of the young nuns walked right into it. You see she had her eyes shut because they were saying the Rosary. Jimmy the ganger was goin' to lift her out but Paddy Mike said 'don't touch her Jimmy, she's a virgin, lift her out with the shovel'. The Reverend Mother herself whipped her out smartly and marched them all back to the convent sharpish. The fact is that all men are banned from that outfit". There was great speculation and great worry about who was going to operate 'the convent farm'; if no men were allowed, who was going to do the work, and would the local men be offered employment. If they can't talk to a man, they argued, how can they offer the work, and how are they going to run the place. This dilemma was solved by Paddy whose sister had just got work in the new work-rooms. She explained that there were three class of nuns. Choir nuns who were referred to as 'mother' and 'sister'. These two categories had to take solemn vows when they were professed. The third category were referred to as lay sisters, and wore a black habit and veil. They took simple vows. They were designated work on the farm, mainly on a supervisory basis. They wore Dutch type clogs, hessian aprons, and were immediately dubbed "slave nuns" by the local people. Eventually a ganger or steward was appointed. He was given accommodation in the former stables which was converted into a cottage. The rest of the men employed there were local and were automatically referred to as "the nuns' men". Their main work was on the convent farm. They cut and saved the turf in the nuns' bog. This was a major task as turf was the main source of heating. They looked after the cattle and the pigs and were responsible for the harvesting of hay and grain. They were closely watched by 'the slave nuns' who firmly believed in getting their pound of flesh from their work force. Very soon 'the nuns' men' discovered how the convent operated. Bells at various intervals summoned the nuns to prayer, or meals or community gatherings. When the cat's away the mice can play, so the men soon looked forward to a little siesta at mantra time. One of them called Frank used to climb the ladder to the hay-shed to have a snooze and a smoke. It was very comfortable and cosy in the soft sweet smelling hay and was a welcome break for ould Frank who had a touch of the rheumatics, especially in winter. One day the Bishop arrived on a visit and prayers were cancelled. The farmyard nun arrived unexpectedly and inquired where ould Frank was. "He's having a kip up in the hay-shed" said a young fella who was bored and wanted a bit of excitement at Frank's expense. She shinned up the ladder as swift as lightning, shouting "Frank, come down here at vonce, you should be working". Alarmed, ould Frank snuggled deeper into the hay and pretended he wasn't there. She was undeterred, she kept calling, and eventually she reached the top and caught Frank red-handed having his illicit break. He couldn't believe his eyes when he saw her. "I vill report you to Reverend Mother, Frank, you are getting paid to vork here, not to lie in hay. She vill 'ave to sack you". Frank was in a fix. He didn't want to lose his job so he had to think fast. "Did I hear ye say ye're goin' to report me to the Reverend Mother, sister. What'll she say when you tell her you were up in the hay-shed with me?" It was her turn to be alarmed. She scampered off and ould Frank never heard a word again about his hay-shed break. He always told this story with great gusto. "I soon put that little furriner in her place" he boasted. "She knew that if she told the Reverend Mother she'd be in bigger trouble than me". "Especially if the Reverend Mother saw what a fine strip of a man you are", said the lad who split on him.

A very important day in the life of the community was the reception of the young postulants into their midst. It was always a memorable and edifying occasion but one day was more memorable than the others, mainly because of gate-crashing or in this case "window crashing" of unwelcome guests.

When the Bride postulants dressed in white received the Holy Habit of the Franciscan Missionaries of Mary, the Bishop, the Canon and other Church dignitaries were invited to the convent to officiate at this important ceremony. The postulants were asked by His Lordship

My child what do you demand?
The Holy Habit of Religion, my Lord . . .
My child you will no longer be known as Mary – but as Sister,
(usually the postulant chose a Saint's name in religion).

The Bishop then blessed the folded habit, girdle and veil, while the Priest answered the prayers. When received and blessed, the white robed Brides rose from the Altar with their folded habits in their open hands, and withdrew, to take off their white dresses and get robed in the beautiful cream habit of St Francis. Traditionally their hair was cut in the crown in the shape of a cross, and they assumed their name in religion, and a dedication to a new life of sacrifice and devotion to God, which ended in Heaven's Court as 'chosen Brides of Christ'. They took the vows of poverty, chastity and obedience. After Mass the 'reception breakfast', a feast worthy of a splendid occasion, and probably the last time the novices would dine with the Bishop, the Priests and their parents, was held in one of the beautiful parlours in the Convent at Loughglynn.

The reception breakfast was always laid in the parlour before the ceremony, as obviously the whole community participated in the joy of the new novices on their great day. The elegant tables were groaning with delicious food, including 'reception cakes' decorated with the religious names of the new novices. There were magnificent white floral displays of lilies, roses, chrysanthemums, whose heady scent filled the air. As the day in question was a glorious summer day all the windows were open, and sunshine filled the Convent lawns lined with ancient beech trees, the lake at times grey and sullen reflected the glorious blue sky and shimmered in the golden light. It was a wonderful day, but alas every silver lining has a cloud. The "travelling people" arrived that morning with their goods and chattels which included goats, donkeys, pie-bald ponies and two 'pedigree' hounds which were named Flora and Fauna. The travelling people arrived on the avenue like clockwork at special times of the year. The animals, including the hounds, were familiar with the terrain. They knew exactly where to look for sustenance. To cut a long story short, the hounds made for the Convent, beheld the

Going to the creamery.

succulent feast, the open windows and no one around, darted through and made short work of the reception breakfast. The Reverend Mother, always outwardly composed, was horror struck and incredulous as she led the Bishop, the clergy and important members of the community into the parlour where the hounds were polishing off the last of the reception breakfast. "Words fail me, my Lord Bishop, Reverend Fathers, Reverend Sisters, parents and novices". The Bishop who had a great sense of humour said, "Don't worry Reverend Mother, it's a great chance for the young novices and indeed all of us to put into practice the virtue of poverty. If it's all the same to you Reverend Mother, we'll have some o' that tasty French cheese that your sisters make in the dairy. I believe it's world famous". Years later I met one of the novices who witnessed the disaster. She was now an experienced missionary sister who had spent years in the leper colonies in India and Pakistan. She often told the story of the reception breakfast debacle at Loughglynn under many a tropic star to the delight of her listeners. "The best part of the story", she said with twinkling eyes, "was that they didn't think anything exciting ever happened at Loughglynn. That's where they were wrong", she said, "where else would you get resourceful hounds who braved the hierarchy of a powerful Church, *and* the Reverend Mother to get themselves a good meal?" We laughed uproariously at the memory. So did the local people at the time who heard the story and told the tale which never lost anything in the telling. It was embroidered and added on to until the original incident was unrecognisable. Like all good tales of course.

When the new creamery was opened, the local farmers came every morning to deliver their milk. They could be seen jogging along at a very early hour in their red and blue painted donkey carts with the shiny creamery cans of milk. They all convened in what was formerly the cobbled court-yard of the Dillon mansion. It was approached through a magnificent crenellated arch-way which was embossed with the Dillon crest. In the landlord's time elegant carriages were kept there. It was also the venue for shooting and fox hunting parties. The 'decoy' wood was used for battues, pheasants, partridges and all game birds were lured and bred there for the annual cull. The mounting stones were used by the grand ladies in their fashionable riding habits to mount the hunters. They can still be seen in the courtyard today. The lazy old donkeys in their brightly painted carts and the easy going farmers exchanging pleasantries with each other as 'the dairy nun' and the young local girls who worked for her separated the cream from the skim or whey. The whey was returned to the farmers and given to the pigs. The finest butter and cheese in Europe was made in the convent at Loughglynn, the recipes were original, rare, and exotic, the cheeses were beyond compare. The local girls learned the art of cheese and butter making from master craftswomen. The other areas where the girls worked and received instruction was the poultry farm. The sisters introduced new breeds of poultry like Rhode Island Reds and White Wyanndots who were excellent table fowl and also productive layers, so the girls gained proficiency in poultry keeping skills and hatching techniques. Dress designing, embroidery, lace-making, crocheting, making altar cloths and vestments for clergy, as well as domestic science were taught in the Franciscan Missionary of Mary workrooms in the convent at Loughglynn. Although the remuneration received by the girls was small they gained diverse skills which stood them in good stead when they emigrated, which of course most of them did — not by choice but by necessity. In the first half of the century 'the avenue' was alive with fair girls riding their bikes and making the road resound with their laugh and glee. The donkey carts with the cheerful farmers and shiny creamery cans and the laughing girls made the avenue a lively, friendly place. Among all this chatter a great character called Ellen who was a "lady gardener" wended her way on foot every day to the convent. Across the years I can still see Ellen smoking her clay pipe, dressed in brown tattered clothes, humming cheerfully to herself and beaming on every one she met on her way to work as if there was no tomorrow. She never missed a day, hail, rain or snow. She plodded on under the whispering trees, a contented happy person. The avenue today is very quiet, no longer is heard the slow clop-clopping of the donkeys egged on by the 'gee-up' there Neddy and the cheerful banter of the farmers as they set the world to rights on the convent avenue, the historic road that once led to "the big house" and was forbidden to the marginalised tenantry on the edge of the woodlands.

Two of the Franciscan sisters taught at Loughglynn school in the first decade of the new century. It was an exciting time as it coincided with the cultural renaissance and a resurgence of interest in the Irish language and Irish culture which was moribund since the famine. Douglas Hyde, a native of Ratra, and a rector's son founded the Gaelic league in 1893. It expanded from 58 branches in 1898 to 600 in 1904, and engaged in a wide educational programme outside the school system, involving Irish language, ceilidh dancing, history and folklore. Hyde was dispirited because so much of the culture was dying and fewer and fewer people were speaking Irish. The children were growing up as English speakers. He knew a storyteller by the name of Sean Cunningham who had been taught thousands of poems from ancient manuscripts as a boy. But he had been sent to a national school and had a stick round his neck and a notch put in it for every word of Irish he spoke at home, and a beating administered at school next day, according to the number of notches. The Gaelic language was aimed to give teachers a knowledge of Irish through all its cultural activities, and bi-lingual programmes were allowed for gaeltacht regions. The school curriculum included elementary science, cookery and laundry. An old auntie used to give us graphic descriptions of school life in Loughglynn under the jurisdiction of the Franciscan missionaries. The dreaded Inspector, or 'the Cigire' of later years, struck terror into the hearts of the teachers. She told us of an impromptu visit by an inspector one afternoon. On his arrival, true to form, he began firing questions at 'the scholars'. The terrified nun teacher was behind him swiftly writing the answers on the blackboard. My aunt who was always an opportunist spotted the nun's 'help' answered all the questions and won herself a gold watch for her "observational skills". She told this story regularly and the watch was proudly displayed in a glass case for all of us to see and admire the concrete evidence of her scholastic attainment. As cookery and domestic science formed part of the curriculum, a domestic science teacher who was referred to as 'the dairy maid' used to come once a week to teach the girls the art of churning and butter making. The chosen girl was responsible for providing a crock of cream. The dairy maid gave them practical lessons on scalding and scrubbing the churn, skimming the cream from the top and churning it into golden butter. The churning was strenuous work. The churn was made by working a plunger called a 'churn-dash' up and down until the cream cracked and specks of butter were formed. When the tiny blobs of butter appeared it was scooped out by hand, thoroughly rinsed with ice cold spring water before it was formed into oblong butter pats, or indeed into any desired shape. The icy crystal clear water helped to solidify the butter. The buttermilk was delicious, a feast in itself. It was handed round in enamel saucepans to the class involved in the churning. Prizes were given for the most artistic efforts (and a girl who later emigrated to America, and made a fortune working in a creamery), created a hen and her chicks from the golden butter as an Easter gift for the parish priest. The sisters left the school before the first world war and it was staffed once more by lay teachers, two of whom were assistant teachers, and two principal teachers, one of them a gentleman. The school was not at this time co-educational. There was a separate boys and girls school divided by iron railings. Two yew trees, one in each playground, formed shelter for the generations of school children who were educated there. The school was amalgamated in the sixties. A new model school was built in Loughglynn village, and mercifully the old school was retained, no doubt always listening and looking at the new trends and the new young Ireland that brought it so much entertainment and history in its chequered past.

CHAPTER FOUR

BERGIN and McDERMOTT

After the Easter rising of 1916 the country was in a state of unrest, and the Sinn Fein election victory in 1918 aroused feelings of patriotism and idealism in the people of Ireland, but especially to the youth. The movement for independence from Britain grew apace, and by 1919 volunteers were being trained throughout the country and ambushes, raids and arrests were commonplace. As the months went by everything went from bad to worse, the country was in a state of chaos and British law broke down as guerrilla war escalated in the south and west. An official report stated that "the principal efforts of Sinn Fein and the Irish volunteers are directed against the Royal Irish Constabulary". In order to counteract this, ex-servicemen from Britain who fought in the Great War were recruited to shore up the R.I.C. The first ex-service men were appointed in January 1920, arriving in Ireland three months later. They were given uniforms made up from parts of army and police outfits, and were immediately dubbed 'the black and tans' after a well known pack of foxhounds. They became notorious. In the course of the struggle for independence an active service unit was formed from the members of the Castlerea battalion of the South Roscommon Brigade of the I.R.A. There were sixteen members in the unit; the Captain was John Bergin, a native of Nenagh, Co. Tipperary. His father was a timber merchant who had an interest in the timber of Mount Druid wood near Ballinagare. He arranged for his son John to be apprenticed to Connolly's timber yard in Castlerea, in order to gain experience for work participation in the family business later on. John joined the Castlerea battalion of the I.R.A. in 1920 and went "on the run". This meant that members were roving guerrilla groups whose objectives were to harass the military and police at every opportunity. When their identity became known to the police, they could no longer stay in their own homes. They were dressed in civilian trench coats and trilby hats, and carried hand guns. They moved across the country by night, wading through marshland, bogs and rivers in all sorts of inclement weather to avoid detection. They slept under hedges, lived off the land, and found shelter in the 'safe houses' of sympathisers. John Bergin was a young man in his early twenties. As a result of his life on the run, he became ill with pleurisy and pneumonia and was taken to the home of Mr Michael O'Callaghan and his wife who looked after him. They also engaged a local nurse, Miss Margaret Coll, later Mrs Mulrennan of Cloonsuck, who was on vacation from the United States, to nurse him back to health. There was a price on his head. Later he was transferred from O'Callaghans to Colls. Whilst he was there, there was a raid by the tans. Bergin was hastily wrapped in blankets, and put in a heated makeshift tunnel which was under-ground at the side of Cloonboniffe Church. His condition worsened and he was moved in stages to Castlebar hospital where he was admitted under an assumed name. He remained there until the end of March 1921, when he discharged himself. He made his way back to Loughglynn to Roger McDermott's safe house on the edge of the demesne.

It was a warm evening in April 1921 when Roger McDermott tramped home with his steeven over his shoulder after 'sticking' a half acre of potatoes in the far field. Rabbits scurried across his path without fear or trepidation and the red sunset promised that the weather was 'set fair' for tomorrow. The yearling calves were munching the sweet new grass in the field by the mearing fence. They were thriving, he thought happily, at least three of them would be ready to sell at the next fair in Ballinlough. The money was badly needed, times weren't good. He reached the long low thatched house; it looked peaceful in the evening light. A few hens were clucking in the farmyard and fussily gathering their chicks about them in preparation for roosting. Roger sat wearily on an upturned pail and scraped the thick limey clay from his boots which were laced with hemp. His brother Martin was milking the cows and he could hear the ping-ping of the frothy milk as it plopped into the milking pail. His sister Maggie was preparing a meal in the house. She was humming "Can anybody tell me where did Staunton's motor go" in between gossiping with Toby, Joe and Steven who were 'on the run' and were having a short respite in the cottage. Despite the tranquil evening, Roger was a troubled man, he lived in troubled times. The 'tan war' with the British was raging, and that night he was hosting the Loughglynn battalion of the boys on the run. He was an easy going, contented man who liked nothing better than chatting with his friends. He was a great story teller. He lived through the landlord regime and witnessed the eviction of a next door neighbour.

The family had to leave McDermott's house when they were forced to emigrate to the United States. This injustice among others etched itself on his mind and at an early age he resolved that Ireland must be free to work outher own destiny. His troubled reverie was broken by a light tap on his shoulder. He jumped nervously It was his friend John Bergin. 'Begob you frightened the heart out o' me, Jack, I thought it was one o' the varmints. You know they're stationed at the workhouse in Castlerea? You're heartily welcome home' he said, pumping his hand. Are the lads here, said Jack? Sure they are, I can't get rid of the blighters, they're in it for the grub. Maggie, he called, come out will ye - look who's here. Maggie ran to the door as she dried her hands on her apron. Arrah, Jack, welcome back, she said as she gave him a big hug. Are you sure you're alright and has your cold gone? You shouldn't have left the 'ospickle'. There's nothing wrong with me, Maggie, that a good square meal won't cure, said Jack, I'm fair clemmed. You could say that again, said Steven and Toby as they made their appearance. Me stomach thinks that me throat is cut, said Toby. Come on in let ye, said Roger, we have a bit o' the pig left over from Christmas, plenty o' cabbage and spuds to spare. The deliciour aroma of bacon and cabbage filled the air. Pull over to the table, said Maggie. I'm ready to dish up. The hungry men placed their caps on their knees and sat down to probably the first squre meal they had in weeks. She plied Bergin with food. Ate up Jack, it'll do you good. It's done me good already to be back, Maggie, among ye all. They were in an optimistic mood, there were tentative rumours of a cease-fire. Gerald (O'Connor) should be here soon, said Bergin. He's attending a meeting of Brigade Staff at Rathconnor, Four-mile house. (The late Gerald O'Connor was a commandant, and a member of the active service unit). He didn't arrive as scheduled, as he took ill and had to stay overnight at his uncle's house (John Crean's in Moyne). They sat round the blazing fire and laughed and talked and caught up with all the gossip. Give us a tune Maggie, said Bergin. I haven't heard a bit o' music or a song for months, it's all gloom and doom. Maggie took down the concertina from a shelf over the chimney-piece and began to play. She was a magic music maker. Where are all the girls, said Jack. Steveneen, go and tell the girls that Jack an' all the lads are here, rarin' to dance. How are they all Maggie, said Bergin. Does Ellie still laugh as much as ever? Ellie with the dancing eyes, he mused. The girls trooped in, jubilant that Bergin, their hero had returned safe and sound. They hadn't seen him for months, and he was always the life and soul of the impromptu dances. Maggie made the rafters ring as they danced the half-sets, lancers and shottiches with

Stephen McDermott.

Joe Satchwell and Toby Scally. Courtesy of the Roscommon Herald.

abandon, after which they gathered round the fire and had a sing-song. Mary Herbert made the tea and passed round the home-made soda bread. They always began the singing with "The Valley of Slievnamon" in honour of Bergin's native county of Tipperary. This was followed by Staunton's Motor Car which was hi-jacked recently by the lads and caused much merriment. Bergin's favourite song was "She Moved through the Fair" (it will not be long love til our wedding day). The latest song was semi-tragic and very near to all their hearts, it was the trumpet of a prophecy. It went like this:

> All around my hat, I wear a tri-coloured ribbon O
> All around my hat until death comes to me
> If anybody asks me why am I wearing it,
> It's all for my true love I never more shall see

They were all in party mood. The girls were full of 'an American wake' which was taking place shortly up the village. All the boys on the run were automatically invited to all 'the hooleys". Suddenly there was a wild keening sound that hushed the revellers. Stephen shivered. Someone's walkin' over me grave, he said, it sounds like the banshee. They say they always keen when 'a Mac' or on 'O' is goin' to die. A chill came over the gathering. Give over Steve, said Joe Satchwell, it's only

Waldron's ould dog cryin' to the moon. Gloom and doom and reality had returned, the girls drifted off with 'we'll see ye tomorrow'. Bergin picked up his rifle which had Captain Peek's name (who was ambushed a few weeks before) inscribed on it. Why don't you get rid of it Jack, my father said, it's a give away. Bergin smiled and climbed the rickety ladder to the loft. Yee'r safe as houses up there, said Dad, as he fastened the shutters. They thought they were safe. The stillness of the spring night was rudely broken by the crying of Waldron's ould dog.

At eight o'clock the next morning, Friday April 19th 1921,

Sean Bergin. O.C. The Flying Column, 1st Batt., South Roscommon Brigade, I.R.A. Killed in action at Loughglynn Wood, 19th April 1921.

Connollys timber yard in Castlerea. The work-shop where John Bergin was apprenticed. Photo courtesy of Ms. Morris.

Roger McDermott went to fodder his cattle. He took the hay-knife from its place on the wall and sharpened it with a scythe-stone. To do this essential job he sat on the doorstep. When he opened the door, the hens and chickens rushed into the kitchen, he scattered Indian meal on the flagged floor and with a clucking sound, they pecked voraciously. As he was sharpening the hay-knife, like every farmer, he looked at the weather, it looked fair set. The sun was peeping above the trees, and the dawn chorus was deafening. I'll finish the sticking in the far field today, thought Roger. He walked to the hay-rick, the sharpened hay-knife swinging in his hand. The yearling stock were looking over the garden fence waiting to be fed. He climbed a short home made ladder to the hay bench and began cutting the rick. The sudden thundering sound of lorries shattered the morning peace and made him jump. He glanced up the ryde - the place was crawling with tans. We're surrounded, he said, caught like rats in traps. He dropped the hay-knife, jumped from the ladder and raced into the house. Maggie was fanning the rakings into a flame to boil the kettle. We're surrounded, he shouted, get the lads out quick. He hammered on the loft with the handle of a pitch-fork. We're surrounded, come on will ye, get out fast. The boys, half dressed, scrambled down the rickety ladder. Bergin had a paroxysm of coughing. He grabbed his rifle and said, keep Steven here, put him back in short pants, he's only a gossoon. Steven followed Bergin. Captain McKay of the Leicester regiment stationed at the workhouse in Castlerea was operating a 'pincer movement' that morning as he led the tans in their 'dance of death'. Bergin and McDermott headed for the north side of the wood. Bergin was very weak. They had hardly gone half a mile when they were stopped and the shooting started. Toby Scally was shot in the thigh, and the impact knocked him into the river. The others got behind the river bank and returned fire. Private Davis was shot in the chest. He was taken to Glynn's house shouting for the "death of the shinner who shot me". The Glynn family who lost their son Pat on active service, cut up white linen sheets to bind the wounds of Private Davis. Joe Satchwell was the first to be struck, a tan bludgeoned him on the back of the head with a rifle butt, then shot him through the foot.

The others turned on Bergin and McDermott and beat them savagely. McDermott was bare footed, the tans pounded his bare feet with rifle butts. A drum head court martial was held and Bergin and McDermott were sentenced to death. Jim Keefe was feeding his cattle in the field adjoining the wood and saw Bergin surrendering his rifle. It belonged to Captain Peek who was previously ambushed by Bergin's unit and had his name engraved on it. He also heard the sentence being read pronounced by Captain McKay. "You are being taken back to be shot in the square in Castlerea as an example."

Satchwell was taken to one of the waiting tenders. Bergin and McDermott were already dead. Satchwell was brought before a court martial in Athlone and sentenced to fifteen years penal servitude. Toby Scally limped to Moyne, he reached Creans which was a suspect house, and was moved from there to Reilly Gallaghers, and then to Joe Jordans in Cootoonmore. Dr Clarke attended him. Roger McDermott came the following night to Jordans and took Toby to Cloonaugh. He was hidden in the well of the side car, the same one which was used to meet the Franciscan nuns when they arrived in Castlerea in 1903. So Toby lived to tell the tale. Later during the Civil War he was taken prisoner in Loughglynn, and interned in Castlebar where he went on hunger stike for eighteen days. he was transferred to Mountjoy gaol and was kept there until the Civil War ended. The late Sister Ann Glynn, who later became a Franciscan Missionary of Mary, braved the tans and ran across the woodlands to alert the clergy that they were needed. The Canon and Fr Donnellan said the last 'amen' as Bergin and McDermott departed from the woodlands and their friends that they loved so well. Ellie Mangan and her cousin Bridget Kelly went to the scene of the shooting. The young tans were still there, they were ordered out of the wood at gun point, but they stood their ground, took photos of the ghastly scene and recorded history. Ellie Mangan leaned against a tall elm tree and with tears pouring down her face, carved the following inscription on the tree trunk.

> In memory of Jack Bergin and Steven McDermott who died fighting to free their country, on Friday April 21st 1921.

And underneath she carved

> All around my hat, I wear a tri-coloured ribbon O
> All around my hat until death comes to me.
> If anybody asks me why am I wearing it,
> It's all for my true love I never more shall see

That inscription was there until the big wind of 1931 toppled the giant elm tree. Over half a century later, the branches of a sapling beech wound itself round the simple cross that commemorates two of Loughglynn's and Ireland's heroes. The wild birds and the whispering leaves sing requiems to Bergin and McDermott who, like Eddie Duffy before them, were waked in another cottage by the wood where they will always be remembered and loved. Always.

On the morning of the shootings the tans stayed behind at our house and held Roger at bayonet point while they interrogated him. Bergin's trilby was hanging on a peg. It had a miniature tri-colour in its brim. "This 'ere is a shinny 'at" screamed a young tan. "That's me ould grandfather's hat, he had it in '98" said dad, "when the ould Queen visited this country. I thought we 'ad a King, said the tan. What 'ave we 'ere, said one bright spark who thought he'd discovered a cache of pikes – the shinners use these for murder. My father tried in between rifle-prods to explain that they were hay-forks used on the farm. Another tan amused himself by taking pot-shots at everything in sight in the yard, hens, ducks, geese and even the old goat tethered to the cross gate. It was a scene of devastation, blood and feathers all over the place. When they tired of this, they took pot-shots at the Sacred Heart picture and the little red lamp (the Sacred Heart lamp) which was burning beneath it, smashed in smithereens on the concrete floor, the flames flared up briefly and then to my dad's relief sputtered out. He fully expected the house to be burned. In the meantime, the relentless interrogation went on as the intermittent sound of gun fire could be heard signalling the death of his friends and comrades. he heard the noise of the Crossley tenders thundering along the ancient ryde, bearing their macabre cargo. Eventually the tans drifted away. Amazingly they didn't find the rifles and ammunition which were hidden under a hay stack in the garden, nor did they find the cartridges which were in the pocket of John Bergin's overcoat. If they had, my father would almost certainly be shot as a collaborator, and the house burned to the ground. The people in the village were sowing potatoes out in the fields on that fateful day. The late Pat Duffy told me that gun fire could be heard in the Aughaderry fields as they all dived for shelter, thinking that the whole village would be under siege as a reprisal. It was a dark, dark day in the history of our village the day Bergin and McDermott were shot.

CHAPTER FIVE

THE MEN AND WOMEN BEHIND "THE HEROES"

The old school was again witnessing high drama. The Demesne hall was used regularly by the tans to frisk and harass the local population. They used to stand them spread eagled against the wall and subject them to a humiliating search. The late Mrs Kelly, our teacher, who was a contemporary of the freedom fighters, used to tell us how they watched these scenes from the classroom windows. The school itself did not escape from the ravages of the invaders. Mr Andrew Keaveney, the principal teacher of the boys' school was harassed by the military. A school girl at the time remembered 'the raids' on the school, 'the master used to abandon his post, jump through the classroom window and escape into the bogs and fields of Driney'. The teachers were often interrogated. During this time the R.I.C. barracks in Loughglynn was burned down. The Sergeant's daughter who was at school in Loughglynn shed bitter tears for her lost home and her lost friends. The war of independence was bitter and bloody and costly. Aughaderry my own village lost two of its finest sons, Pat Glynn and Ned Shannon. Aughadriston our neighbouring village lost Michael Carty. Stephen McDermott was a native of Tully near Ballinagare. John Bergin used to claim with pride that he was born between the Galtees and Slievenamon. They were all young men full of promise. Loughglynn paid dearly for its sons who fought and died so bravely in its lush woodlands. The freedom fighters were backed up, and had the support of sympathisers in the local population. Without the cooperation of these people the war would never have been won. The 'safe houses' as we have seen were especially vulnerable, the people lived on a knife edge, there was always the odd 'informer' who gave vital information to the invading army. Nevertheless they welcomed and sheltered the young men when they were 'on the run' They provided bases for their exploits; they travelled with risky dispatches, and had been just as heroic as the fighters. They suffered severe financial and emotional loss and many of them were bankrupted. The Loughglynn women, many of whom were members of 'Cumann na mban' also played a major part in winning the war. The late Mrs Margaret Mangan - 'Maggie' and her four daughters, Mary-Kate, Bridgie, Annie and Ellie welcomed the freedom fighters into their home and supported them unstintingly. Without this support the movement would not have been the success it was. Shortly before she died Mary Kate Mangan proudly showed me the medals which she was given in recognition of her work as a guerrilla activist in Donegal. As children of the revolution we got a first hand account of the action; however, there were some areas that were still kept secret even half a century later. I knew there was a tunnel in one of the

Mrs Margaret Mangan, M. K. Mangan.

back gardens, an emergency escape route. I asked her about this but she refused to divulge this information. I made a promise - I won't break it she said. Annie, Ellie and Maggie were interrogated and harassed for hours on the day of the shootings. The tans threatened to burn the house down and they were ordered to give them meals at bayonet point. The girls and their mother attempted to move the furniture into the barn where the volunteers drilled, and where a young British soldier was held hostage for a considerable time, but they were stopped and threatened at gun-point. They heard the

Roger McDermott and Mrs Margaret Mangan in 1950.

Mary Kate Mangan and her mother Maggie in the 50's

vicious shootings in the woodlands, and the thundering noise of the Crossley tenders, manned with bayoneted tans, carrying their macabre cargo along the ancient tree lined ryde. Jim Keefe who was an eye witness from behind his hedge, said that the heads of Bergin and McDermott bumped on the stone ryde as they thundered along. The Mangans' were devastated, their young friends who represented hope and promise for the future were dead. Things would never be the same again.

In the meantime Bridgie Mangan who worked at E.J. McDermotts in Castlerea heard with trepidation about the shootings in Loughglynn. The Crossley tenders thundered into the square in Castlerea and immediately all sorts of rumours

Left to right: Mary Kate Mangan, Brigid Mangon, Roger Keaveney, Brigid Kelly and Ellie Mangan.

floated around, such as "The rebels were found in a widow's house in the woods at Loughglynn, the widow and her family were arrested, the house was burned down". Bridgie was extremely distressed, she had no way of finding out the real story, nor could she leave her post at E.J's where political discussions were frowned on. At closing time, she cycled home madly. When she reached the avenue there were still pockets of tans stopping and searching the local population. The ryde was still guarded by the military. Eventually she reached home and heard the heart breaking story Only the night before they danced and sang and laughed with their young friends, and planned future parties and 'hooleys'. Ellie Mangan was a very close friend of John Bergin - it was said they were engaged to be married. Bridgie who was a fine needlewoman and dress designer, made the tricolour flags which draped the coffins of Bergin and McDermott. What happened to the brave girls and women who made history and who were generally unsung? Bridgie and Annie Mangan emigrated to America. Bridgie married an American, Annie married an Irish emigrant from Donegal. Ellie died at the age of twenty four, she never recovered from the death of her lost love. Mary Kate returned to Aughaderry and worked with her mother Maggie (who died in 1960). She herself died a few years ago in the Convent at Loughglynn, where many of her friends, including Sister Ann Glynn and Sister Ellie Kate Mangan were nuns. So the Loughglynn women played a major part in the shaping of the nation, many of them considered themselves combatants, not mere auxiliaries in the revolution. Sadly the importance of their contribution was rarely acknowledged.

> The singer sings a rebel song
> And everybody sings along
> Just one thing I'll never understand
> Every damn rebel seems to be a man
> For he sings of 'the Bold Fenian men'
> and the boys of the Old Brigade,
> What about the women who stood there too
> "When history was made".
>
> Brian Moore, *Invisible Women*

THE GANDER AND THE BLACK-AND-TAN

However, the tan war wasn't all gloom and doom, it had its lighter side. Even people who weren't sympathetic to 'the cause' always backed 'the lads' against the oppressors who were at a serious disadvantage. Irish humour helped the people enormously to survive the onslaughts of the tans. This was a powerful safety valve and a boost for morale. The lads on the run weren't always in the good books of the clergy, some of whom didn't approve of their tactics and strategies. The volunteers didn't agree with the sentiments of the clergy but at the same time they had a great respect for their faith, and desperately wanted to practise it. They were on the horns of a dilemma.

Margaret Mangan's 'safe house' as it is today.

One young volunteer who frequently stayed at our house told how he went to Confession full of trepidation, as he was in an ambush and shot a tan. He prepared a long list of the usual sins ready for the priest - missing the Holy Sacrifice of the Mass on Sunday, missing his prayers, cursing, calling God's name in vain, being disrespectful to his parents, kissing his girl at the gable end. At the end he blurted out 'an' I killed a tan, Father, at the ambush beyant'. He was waiting for the tirade from the priest and the refusal of absolution, when he heard the gentle voice of the priest saying, "It isn't necessary to confess your venial sins my son". You could have knocked me down with a feather, he said, I couldn't believe me ears. From that day on the gentle priest was kept busy hearing the confessions of the boys 'on the run'.

Big Bill Cartwright, a vicious 'auxie' terrorised the countryside. He went round with an arrogant swagger and a mouth like a torn pocket. He loved terror for terror's sake. The people described him as 'the manest of the mane – the scum of the earth'. He used to swagger round with three revolvers stuck in his belt and a gun slung across his shoulders. When he wasn't bragging about all 'the huns' he killed at Wipers (Ypres) he was boasting about shooting 'shinners' and keeping 'lor and order' in this god-forsaken land. He always stood in the Crossley tenders – huge legs apart like some great Colossus, as the tans and auxies rampaged round the countryside, blazing indiscriminately to right and left. But like all bullies, he was about to meet his match, as he and his minions were rampaging past Bid Quinn's cottage. It was a small two roomed house with a thatched roof, the outhouses were attached and there was a cobbled yard at the front, surrounded by a fuchsia hedge. Although Bid was doubled up with the rheumatics she was a very thrifty housewife. She always had eggs and butter for 'the eggler' or travelling shop man, and she was very proud of a clutch of chickens newly hatched as they pecked round the farmyard with the Rhode Island red mother hen. It took her all year to coax the temperamental Rhode Island to 'clock' (brood) and then she kept getting off the nest. The neighbours swore that Bid made ould Pakie take turns with the hen to sit on the nest to keep the eggs warm until the chicks were hatched. He'd as soon see the tans coming as Bid. "No wan else has this class o' hen" bragged Bid, "they're a new breed from Amerikay — great layers. I'll be made up with them". Man proposes but Big Bill disposes, hens and chickens were a favourite target of the tans. They took pot shots at them. Big Bill spotted the chickens and killed every one of them. "We'll do the same to the shinny b'stads" he shouted. Bid was beside herself with rage. She hobbled after them with a long handled brooom, shrieking "God blast ye to hell, ye black hearted divils – Hell won't be full until ye're all . . ." She didn't finish. The tender ground to a halt so fast that the screenings on the road were scattered all over the place. Bid was covered in dust and pebbles and began hobbling backwards as Big Bill ran towards her, guns poised menacingly. He had a grin on him, like a dead hare, said Bid, as he stuck a revolver in me face. He'd have murthered me as sure as eggs is eggs, said Bid, only for the gander, followed by a flock of geese rushed out of the farm-yard like bats out of hell, squawking like demons and flapping their wings viciously. It was a surprise attack. They made straight for Big Bill — the gander in murderous mood, hissing and snapping at his heels as he ran back to the tender, screaming 'the bleedin' banshees are after me — get movin' quick. His minions were falling about laughing, the neighbours all came out to see the fun. Both side, tans and people for once, were on the same side, laughing and jeering at Big Bill's downfall as he was dragged into the Crossley. The big bully had met his match. Bid Quinn's gander had become a hero overnight. He made up for the awful loss of Bid's American chicks. Like all heroes, he was immortalised in song.

> Oh, can anybody tell me where did Biddy's gander go,
> It wasn't down to Ballagh town, nor over to Mayo,
> No, he frightened Big Bill Cartwright, the auxie with the guns,
> An damn near nearly kilt him when he bit the bastard's bum

CHAPTER SIX

THE CIVIL WAR

The Civil War has been one of the darkest chapters in Irish history. In our house it was never discussed, like the famine it was too painful. As children of the revolution we identified with the young freedom fighters, the ballads written in their honour were our nursery rhymes. The Civil War was a grey area. When Michael Collins was assassinated at Beal na mblath in his own County, the heart went out of the Irish people, disillusionment set in, and a malaise settled over the land.

The Treaty negotiations began in London on 11th October 1921. After months of bargaining, Lloyd George the British Prime Minister, threatened the Irish delegation if they failed to sign, with a return to war. Michael Collins and his coleagues agreed to Lloyd George's plan to partition Ireland as proposed in a Government of Ireland bill 1920. The bill provided for a parliament in the south of twenty-six counties and a northern parliament of six. It fell short however of the hoped for Republic that so many Irish people voted for. Collins wrote of his anguish:

"Think — what have I got for Ireland? Something which they had wanted these past 700 years. Will anyone be satisfied at the bargain? Will anyone? I tell you this — early this morning, I signed my death warrant. I thought at the time how odd, how ridiculous — a bullet may just as well have done the job five years ago".

The new state was to be known as the Irish Free State, or 'Saorstat Eireann'. It was said that a Telegraph messenger lad in Dublin, incorrectly and rudely translated it as "Sore arse Erin" when he first saw the motif on a stamp. Feelings in Ireland ran deep over the Treaty, many felt that the delegates should have stuck out for a Republic, others especially business people and the Church wanted peace. D'ail Eireann ratified the Treaty by just 64 votes to 57. In mid January 1922 a provisional government was set up headed by Michael Collins. By now the I.R.A. had split and pro-Treaty section formed the new Free State Army. The Anti-Treatyites (later known as irregulars) set up a separate headquarters at the Four Courts building in Dublin. In the early hours of 28th June 1922, the Free State army using artillery supplied by the British attacked the Republican head-quarters. The conflict over the Treaty both inside and outside the Dail split the country in two. The Civil War raged for ten months, ending in April 1923, with the Republican Army admitting defeat. This left lasting divisions in Irish politics for decades to come. The following headlines are taken from the Freeman's Journal. They give an indication of the course of events in the Loughglynn, Castlerea, Ballaghaderreen areas.

WEST
MAYOS TIME OF TRIAL
'Effects of irregular occupation'
Ruined homes. Arrests: aged people starving: 20.7.22

BALLYHAUNIS TAKEN
'CASTLEREA WELCOMES THE NATIONAL TROOPS'
All the towns of Connaught cleared of "the irregulars"

BALLAGHADERREEN EVACUATED
Irregulars in Flight 8.7.22
"While cherishing undying gratitude for your services and appreciation of your position, <u>ROSCOMMON</u> DEMANDS WITH PRACTICAL UNANIMITY THE RATIFICATION OF THE

TREATY"
V.Rev. Canon Cummins to E. de Valera
(Cork Weekly Examiner 7.1.22)

The Civil War raged for ten months, as former friends and comrades turned the guns on each other. Families were rent in two, brother fought against brother, and fathers against sons. It ended in April 1923 with the Republican Army admitting defeat. The ominous albeit occasional sound of gunfire could be heard sputtering ominously across the ruined countryside. The intellectual, political and cultural life of the county was decimated. The country was in a state of depression and unease. The ghost of the Civil War kept rattling and clanking, and in the coming years was used to emphasise the roots of the two main parties, Fianna Fail and Fine Gael. I vividly recollect election addresses in my youth; the bedrock of these speeches were a litany of the bravery or the sacrifices of members of the party during 'the troubles'. The economy was rarely an issue, even though unemployment was rife and the only option for the youth was the emigrant ship. There was considerable damage to bridges, roads and rail lines during the War of Independence, and the Civil War added at least £30 million to these losses. Communications were destroyed, trade and industry severely damaged, and many businesses collapsed. This was the battered face of the birth of infant state as it screamed and kicked its way into a fragile existence. The people had to pick up the pieces and make the best of the meagre resources that they had. As in all wars, ultimately it is the people who pay the piper. After the death of Collins, Mulcahy quickly reassured the Free State forces and Cosgrave was given the chairmanship of the provisional government. He was helped by Kevin O'Higgins, Minister of Economic Affairs. Mulcahy was appointed Commander in Chief and Minister for Defence. Cosgrave's comment on the death of Collins stated that "His death has sealed his work, and before the tragedy of his death the nation is resolved to bring the work to triumph". The people paid the price of the Civil War by seeing families split almost to this very day. The people had to suffer severe economic stagnation, emigration was increased a hundred fold, and continued unabated until the end of the sixties when there was a slight decline. Most damaging of all was the legacy of bitterness that is only now — eighty years on — declining. The Free State (Saorstat Eireann) had no national debt when it was set up, but ended the Civil War with little or no resources, and facing colossal costs. The Civil War was fought basically for an ideal, "A Republic". In 1949 it was declared a Republic by the then Taoiseach John A. Costello, and opted out of the Commonwealth without a shot being fired.

CHAPTER SEVEN

THE LEAN YEARS

The Civil War ended officially in May 1923, when Frank Aiken issued an order to dump arms. There was however no negotiated cease-fire, and Free State troops continued for some time to search for arms and to make arrests. Prisoners were released slowly. The new Civic Guards who were unarmed under Eoin O'Duffy had extreme difficulty in maintaining law and order, especially in areas of continued unrest. Land theft carried out at random by armed groups was a major problem, and administration was practically non-existent.

De Valera was anxious to keep the notion of a republic alive, in order to do this he stated that anti-Treaty candidates should fight in the August 1923 election which was to end the provisional government, and officially set up 'The Free State'. Initially de Valera's party policy was not to recognise the state at all, but he argued "The more progress we make in the coming elections, the more certain will be our victory at subsequent elections, the elections give an opportunity of explaining our party's policy, and reaching the people which I think should be availed of." At the election the Free State party which was now called "Cumann na Gaedheal" had gained 64 seats to the Republican 44. It was a good omen for de Valera who founded a new party, "Fianna

Fail" in 1923, when he entered the Dail, breaking completely with "Sinn Fein". This action was forced upon him by an electoral amendment act that required every intending Dail candidate to swear an affidavit, and take the oath of elected. De Valera signed, and called it "an empty formula". On 16th February 1932 the country voted for a change, 'Fianna Fail' gained 16 seats, 'Cumann na nGaedheal' lost 9. De Valera's long political reign had begun. He fought and won the election against a background of unemployment, slum housing, poverty, emigration, and a general malaise and disillusionment that swept across the land. De Valera capitalised on statements made by the Free State government while in power to help him to win the 1932 election. The minister for industry and commerce, Mr McGilligan in the Free State government stated that "People may have to die in this country, and may have to die from starvation . . . If it is said that the government has failed to adopt effective means to find useful work for willing workers, I can only answer that it is no function of government to provide work for anybody". This was a powerful propaganda weapon in de Valera's bid for power. When he entered the Dail in 1932, he took a salary cut, this he said was following in the footsteps of James Connolly whose ambition was to give "the workers of Ireland the living they were entitled to in their own country". The sort of living de Valera envisaged was, he said, "decent frugal living" and defending his own protectionist policies he argued that "over eighty thousand people could be employed in manufacturing and producing goods that we import unnecessarily".

The 1932 election campaign was a very colourful and exciting affair. De Valera made several personal appearances in country towns. My father told us about his triumphal entry into the square in the town of Ballagh. He was met by, and escorted in by a local volunteer cavalry, whose horses' manes were braided and intertwined with green, white and orange ribbons – the republican colours.

The music was provided by a fife and drum band. The crowds clapped and cheered themselves hoarse. They all joined in the latest hymn of adulation to de Valera.

> It's up de Valera, the rebels as well,
> It's up dear old Ireland, and England to hell,
> Release our bold prisoners, that's plain to be seen,
> For these are our colours, white, orange and green.

I was four years old at the time, and I can vaguely remember my father and mother decorating the mane of our horse in the republican colours, and then riding it into town (my mother riding pillion) to join the de Valera cavalcade and pay obeisance to their "chief". When they returned home, my father said "Dev looked like a king in command clothed in a flowing black cloak, riding on his white horse". We have 'a new Parnell' he said proudly. That evening de Valera was escorted out of town with a torch-light procession. The dawn had come at last, euphoria was everywhere, the people said under Dev "every man is entitled to a living in his own country". Times are going to get better. Years later a neighbour who was a boy when Dev visited Ballagh, and who was there with his own parents commented, "The people were poverty stricken, they were ill clad, ill fed, and their boots were broken, most of my friends were barefoot". I wondered to this day what they were cheering for, 'the frugal living era' had begun. The economic war with Britain was triggered off by de Valera after taking legal advice on the 1926 document which confirmed the financial agreement of 1923 between the British and Irish governments, in which the Irish had agreed to pay the full amount of the annuities. The first item in the ultimate financial settlement stated, "The Government of the Irish Free State, undertake to pay to the British Government at agreed intervals, the full amount of the annuities accruing from time to time under the Irish land acts 1891–1909, without any deduction whatsoever on account of income tax or otherwise". De Valera refused to pay the annuities. An official record stated that during his meeting in Downing Street, London,

> de Valera made it clear that he wished to go behind the two agreements of 1923 and 1926 stating that he was of an opinion that a fair settlement would not merely leave the Irish Free State under no liability to make any payment, but would require the

British government to pay a considerable sum to the Irish Free State.

De Valera stormed out of the meeting and the economic war began. The annuities were not paid. The British imposed the 28% levy. The Irish responded with similar levies imposed on British goods coming into Ireland. At one stage de Valera stated that his market had gone forever.

The effect of the tariff blizzard hit agricultural exports very badly, mainly cattle, butter, eggs and pigs. During my first year at school I remember my father taking four calves to the fair in Ballagh. He promised us all he'd buy us sandals for the summer. He returned with the sandals, brown canvas with rubber soles. I was over the moon. They looked great, but he sold the calves for a half-a-crown a head in order to purchase the sandals. I heard him say that a calf's skin was worth more than its carcass. The bigger farmers suffered very badly as the livestock prices plummeted, and their assets disappeared before their eyes. The calves by this time were virtually unsaleable, (the cattle jobbers wouldn't even bid for them at the fairs), so de Valera in his infinite wisdom ordered them to be slaughtered, and free meat given to the poor. Nobody wanted to be described as 'poor' so even if you were eligible for "free beef" you didn't pretend you were. My mother overheard two women gossiping one day, "You'll never believe this Maggie, I met 'high and mighty' Nora Green this morning come from town and she had a bulging shopping bag o' beef on the carrier of her bike. She jumped off to bid me the time o' day and the bag burst and all the beef scattered all over the road". '. . . Nora, ye never let on ye're on the 'free beef', I said. She didn't know where to put herself. Any road, she didn't get much o' that because all the dogs in the country had it ate in a minute. We never got any of the free beef bonanza and up to this very day I wonder why we didn't. De Valera increased public spending by 20%. The dole, which amounted to a derisory half a crown a week (25p today) gradually increased to five shillings (50p). Families were large and apart from this pittance there was nothing coming in. Road works were started, (reminiscent of famine times), the work was divided between carters and labourers. A ganger was in charge of all the workers, and a county engineer would occasionally swoop down to make sure that they got their pound of flesh. The road work was very temporary. Carters were given a fortnight's work and then laid off, to give other men a chance to be employed. However, if you voted Fianna Fail, "de Valera's political bandwagon", you had a chance of extra work if you were in 'the know' and had in the jargon of the day 'pull'. The Councillors were the best people to approach, and I have seen men coming home from a hard day's work drenched to the skin, having got the sack and who were faced with the prospect of walking four or five miles to an "influential" Councillor to plead with him to give them extended work. It was a pitiable state of affairs. The quarry in Driminagh was opened and all the stones and screenings for the road works were quarried there. The workmen used to congregate in Mangan's house at lunch time for their dinner break. I remember the sticks of gelignite used for blasting which were placed all around the hearth in order to make it more pliable. Amazingly we were never blown up. Another means of making ends meet was selling loads of hay in Ballyhaunis. My father used to load the hay the night before, and set off at five o'clock in the morning for the market in the square at Ballyhaunis. The hay used to fetch about 5/- (25p) a hundredweight; it was weighed on the square, the buyers usually came from the Aughamore, Glann, Charlestown and Kilkelly areas. My father, or any other seller, would then have to set off to the buyer's home in or around the areas mentioned to deliver the hay. He generally arrived home well after midnight - a long day and night by any standards, for low remuneration. It was the best of times, it was the worst of times. Materially we weren't very prosperous, but we were very secure in a loving environment. Certain bills had to be paid 'on the dot'. We all knew that the brown envelope with the red Saorstat Eireann motif spelled trouble. It began with the unfamiliar "A Chara" greeting. This puzzled the older generation as they never learned Gaelic at school. I heard an old neighbour say, "What does it all mane? I know the first bit says 'Our Charlie' but I'm damned if I know who Miss Lemeas is" – the demand notes ended with 'Mise le

Meas', a great term of esteem. They rapidly changed the Celtic endearment to a menacing red "FINAL NOTICE", the language of the ancient enemy if these demands weren't promptly met. The rates and the rate collector were another menace when it was time to meet the rate bills we used to offer up the Rosary so that we could sell the cattle to pay the bill. If the fair was bad the rate collector was dodged. He used to collect the money outside the church, so it was fairly easy to elude him by taking the Mass walk through the wood and the Sandy Road. It was only a matter of time until he had to be paid. It was a prestigious job, nearly all the local government jobs were Fianna Fail nominees and were very sought after. Times were difficult but the people were resilient and never lost their sense of humour which was the safety valve of the nation at the time. The "gangers" sometimes were drafted in from other areas to oversee a big job like the tarmacadaming of the main road from Ballagh to Castlerea. Some of them were hard task-men. Part of the job was to make sure that each cart load of screenings and sand or stones was measured and recorded. If the measurement didn't meet the prescribed standards, the workers' pay would be docked, or reduced. The gangers themselves were terrified of the Engineer who pounced at regular intervals. One of the gangers who my father described as being 'one of the decentest men in Ireland', had a great love for 'a drop o' the cratur' at any time of the day. One frosty morning he went well over the limit to keep out the cold. The men said you didn't have to look out for him, you could smell him a mile away. To make bad matters worse, the chug, chug of the Engineer's new Baby Austin could be heard in the distance. I'm done for, said Bill the Ganger. Hould on, said Dad. He nipped in smartly to Cafferky's (the door was never locked). Mary Kate and Patrick were out, so he took the quarter of tea from the mantel piece, dashed out and said "open your mouth Bill, quick" and stuffed the dry tea in. "Chew it, an divil a thing he'll notice Bill". Bill chewed and swallowed. The other workers tipped a load of screenings in front of the Engineer's car so he couldn't move. Bill continued to chew his way through the tea and was as sober as a judge when the Engineer finally reached him. At break time Dad went into Cafferkys in order to explain about the missing tea. Mary Kate met him at the door. "You'll never believe this, Roger. I can't give you any tay today, some young blackguard came in while we were out and stole the tay from the mantelpiece. That's the youth today for you, no respect for anything or anyone. They wouldn't do that when we were young". When my mortified dad eventually got a word in edgeways, he had to tell them that he was 'the blackguard' who stole the tay, but explained that Bill the ganger had sent one of the young lads to Loughglynnn to buy her another quarter o' tay, to replace it. Even today, if I smell boiling tar, I'm back again on 'the hog road' of my childhood watching all these men tarmacadaming it, and laughing and joking about de Valera's new Ireland where there was going to be jobs and 'frugal living' for all.

While the men folk were out earning a crust, the women as usual were keeping the home fires burning brightly. It was the custom at the time that wives and mothers worked inside and outside. They referred to it as 'workin ithin and ithout'. Families were large, from once the children were able, they were allotted tasks. In our house my mother was mainly responsible for milking the cows, feeding the calves, looking after the sow and bantams, and feeding them. The hens, chickens, geese, ducks and turkeys were also the province of the housewife. In addition, they helped in the fields in spring time and harvest time. They also reared the turf on the bog from the moment it was cut until it was dry enough to clamp. When it was eventually carted home to the garden for winter fire fuel, they 'freed' it which was an art in itself. They were, of course, responsible for the everyday running of the house. The facilities were nil. It was pre-electricity, pre-gas, and pre-running water. The turf fire therefore was the main source of energy. It was used for heating the house, cooking for the family, boiling water for wash day, boiling pig feed and mashes for the animals. I remember massive iron pots of potatoes being hoisted on a crane by my mother and lifted off when they were boiled. The potatoes were then strained and pounded with oatmeal, bran or other kind of mash to feed the pigs and hens. The hens were a viable asset. If they were good layers they provided a much needed monetary asset for the housewife. The eggs were sold either to 'the eggler', a travelling shop man or taken to the local shops in the village. With the change of government in 1932 there were also changes in regulations about food hygiene. For instance, all eggs had to be washed before they were sold. I was nearly always given the task of washing the eggs. I hated it. The eggs were placed in a basin of luke-warm water and after I had scraped the bits of straw and droppings of them, I had to take them out one by one and rub them gently with bicarbonate of soda in order to remove any stains. I got a penny if I managed to clean fifty without any breakages. If I broke or cracked one I got told off. In springtime my mother was always on the look out for broody hens, "clockers". When she send us children to a neighbours house up the village with a clutch of eggs, about a dozen and one for luck. The eggs would be exchanged for a clutch from the neighbour who had a good breed of cockerel when the chicks were eventually hatched they would be strong and healthy. It was a great joy and wonder to us children to see the fluffy yellow chicks breaking through their zig-zag shell. We used to stroke their silky fluffy down then gently hold them in our palms and encourage them to peck. The "poultry lady", another government official changed this somewhat. She advised housewives to 'order' day old chicks from some poultry factory or other, and rear them under an aladdin type lamp that smelt terribly of paraffin oil, and gave no comfort whatsoever to the little fluffy chicks cheeping and panicking who huddled around it for warmth looking in vain for their mother. Understandably the chicks died one by one from sheer misery. No wonder, no comforting cosy wing to shelter them. My mother threw out the lamp and reverted to the tested and tried method, "the clocker". To our delight our miracle chicks had returned. In the springtime, as well as the chicks all the other young animals were born. We had a sow who presented us with ten or eleven bonhams every spring. As children we used to watch as the baby pigs were born one by one. They were perfect, white in colour at first and gradually changing to pink as my mother rubbed them briskly with straw, and placed them in our hands as we led them squeaking feebly to their mother's teats. We always had a fire in the barn for this occasion and we used to stay up all night to watch over them at the early stages, lest the sow with her great bulk inadvertently lay on one of them and smothered it. When they were three months old or thereabouts they were taken to the market in Ballagh to be sold. The market depended on demand and like the calves, if demand wasn't there we took the bonhams back or sold them for undervalue. We always kept one to fatten up for Christmas, which was pig killing time, and almost as festive as the feast itself. This was a ritual which took two to three days. First the pig was slaughtered, the blood was kept in a large basin to make black and white puddings, using the pig's intestines. The pig was then hung up generally on our back door with a huge potato in its mouth. It was a frightening apparition to watch on a dark winter's night. The boning and curing of the bacon then took place. We generally ended up with two sides of bacon which was carefully salted and placed in a bacon box. Later when the curing process was completed, the sides were hung from a large hook in the ceiling. The turf smoke which had an elusive aroma of wind and heather helped in the curing process, and gave us delicious crispy bacon for the rest of the winter. Killing and curing one's own bacon is not an option in the economy based Ireland of today, they don't know what they're missing. Making the black puddings was an art in itself, it sounds barbaric but the end result was haute cuisine. The pig's blood was placed in a big iron pot, herbs, mainly sage, onions, chives and cereal oatmeal were all mixed together and boiled until the mixture thickened. Rendered lard from the pig was also added. It was thoroughly mixed and looked very similar to a witches' brew. The puddings (or guts) were thoroughly cleansed in boiling salted water. I can still see my mother turning them inside out to make sure they were totally hygienic. When the mixture was ready, it was cooled and the puddings were filled. They were then boiled slowly in a pot of boiling water. When they were finally cooked, they were cooled off and made a scrumptious meal with ham and eggs. The head of the pig was boiled into a jelly substance and made into "brawn". This was traditionally used in spring time for sandwiches, especially in the bog. So every bit of the pig was used except his squeak. I hated the brawn.

The fire was the hub of the home, the very heart that everything revolved around. It was the focus for all the family occupying almost a wall in its own right, the blazing soaring flames in between two hobs, all its accoutrements, the iron kettle, the big pots, the skillet, the bread oven, all suspended by hooks on the crane was very comforting and reassuring. On winter nights it was round the fireside that we sat and talked with ourselves and our neighbours. It was round the warm hearth that we sang songs and played music. It was round the fire that local history and folklore was passed on to us, it was there that we learned the secrets of the fairy forts, the round towers, the Chieftains and Kings of old and naturally the injustices of the invader. My mother made her own bread, everyone did at that time. Shop loaves were only bought once a week. I can still see my mother across the years standing at the kitchen table making the cakes, expertly mixing the flour with the soda, and pouring the fresh buttermilk into the well in the centre. After the mixing she kneaded the mixture into cake form, sprinkled it with flour and cut the shape of the cross on it before placing it in the hot oven on the hearth. Soon the delicious aroma of the baking bread filled the kitchen, and even now I can never pass a bakery without a feeling of nostalgia for the fleeting simple joy of childhood and an era that has gone for ever. The bag of flour (112 lbs) in the corner near the fire with the picture of a woman - arms outstretched to the rays of the rising sun was very reassuring. Underneath this vision was something that said "this is a product of Ballisodare flour mills". The flour bags which were made of the finest cotton were washed and bleached, sewn together and made into sheets. We had no electricity, so oil lamps were the only light we had. This was another chore that my mother had to do each evening. She filled the lamp with oil, cleaned the barrel and trimmed the wick, finally she cleaned the globe until it shone. Her wedding ring glinted in the firelight and made a pleasing tinkling sound as she burnished the glass. Years later when rural electrification was introduced I used to visit an old lady who had it installed. I was very puzzled as she still used the old oil lamp. "Isn't the electricity working Biddy?", I said. "Arrah it is", she said, "but I only put it on to light the lamp".

We had of course no running water but we had a wonderful spring well close to the house, the water which was crystal clear and icy cold used to gurgle up from the depths of the earth, a long way down flickering in its dark green mossy bed fringed with fauna. My mother used to fill two white pails with water while we followed behind her with ten sweet cans full. This supply of water generally lasted until evening. Today, sadly, our lovely well that seemed to hold so many secrets in its lucid depths is badly polluted and no running water today can compare with the delicious iciness and purity of the water in the well that served us so well during our childhood years. I am also aghast to see the exorbitant prices that are charged today for bottled water which usually has a fizzy, artificial taste, and I sigh for the old well.

Budgeting was very difficult in the hungry years, as money was in extremely short supply. [The economic slump was universal, of course]. The main problem was unemployment, and the continued economic war crippled the livestock market. There was no income to talk about, and bringing up a family even in remotely frugal comfort was difficult to say the least. There was no family allowance and the dole, which was a miserly pittance, was means-tested. The protected market ensured that the entrepreneurs had no competition, and the trademark 'Deanta in Eirinn' was as often as not a hall-mark for shoddy goods. To exacerbate matters, there was a universal slump. Times were bad in the United States and in Britain as well, so the emigrants who sent remittances home were badly hit. This was on top of the heart-break and disillusionment of the civil war. De Valera's dream of "a land bright with cosy homesteads, whose fields and villages would be joyous with the sounds of industry, with the romping of sturdy children, the contests of athletic youths, the laughter of comely maidens, whose fireside would be forums for the wisdom of old age", failed to materialise. Sadly, in order to make dreams happen some practical steps are necessary. It was easy for de Valera from his vantage point in his luxurious home in Dublin to envisage an idyllic Ireland, a magic Tirnonogue ruled over by a kind 'Taoiseach'. The story was somewhat different for the rest of his countrymen, who had to face and live through the stark realities of an almighty depression, whose fields and villages were certainly not joyous with the sounds of industry, the laughter of comely maidens, might have been heard in workplaces of Britain's cities like London, Birmingham, Liverpool, Manchester and Leeds, if they were lucky enough to secure any kind of employment at all. As the end of the hungry thirties approached, Britain declared war on Germany, and neutral Ireland's 'emergency' years began.

CHAPTER EIGHT
THE EMERGENCY IN LOUGHGLYNN

It was Spring in 1939, we were playing in the school playground when we heard a thunderous noise, an aeroplane was flying low over our school. It was the first time we had seen a plane, it was like a giant bird in the sky. Our teacher who was as excited as we were said 'If England and Germany go to war, aeroplanes will be a familiar sight, this war is going to be fought in the air'. It was the trumpet of a prophecy. In September 1939 England declared war on Germany when the British Prime Minister Chamberlain's appeasement policy failed, and 'Peace in our time' declaration fluttered into the dustbins of history. De Valera decreed that Eire, as it was known under the 1937 Constitution, was to remain neutral. It could be argued that Ireland's freedom began in 1939. It was the first time in 700 years that she was totally alone and neutral.

In 1939 Eire was an Infant State barely seventeen years old, "the terrible beauty" that was born in 1916, the murders and atrocities carried out by the Black and Tans, the heartbreak and disillusionment of the Civil War spawned a new Ireland that still had vestiges of its colonial past but was determined to forge its own new culture. The schools were an ideal place to start. The Irish language was introduced and formed a major part of the national curriculum, even though many of the teachers were unfamiliar with the language and had to learn it themselves. The big houses of the former ascendancy crumbled and decayed, grass growing on avenues, and flaking paint on once elegant windows and doors. Many of the mansions were burned during the troubles, and some ascendancy families had chosen to leave the country altogether.

The war years in neutral Ireland could be described as a time warp, in fact time went backwards. Life became inward looking, isolated and self absorbed. Nevertheless in 1939 Ireland was clean, uncluttered and peaceful. The first intimation of war in Britain was the return of emigrant families who had settled in England's cities and returned to the safety of their homeland. It was a traumatic homecoming. I remember young Irish girls in tears because they had to break up the home and families that they worked so hard for and settle in cramped accommodation in their parents' home. They were afraid of the bombs, the bullets, the air raids and the call up. They brought excitement and a breath of fresh air to the Irish countryside. At that time there were very few radio sets to be found in the villages of Ireland. The visitors had the very latest Marconi models. They were operated on batteries which had to be charged periodically. This was done at a garage, and it was very prestigious to dangle the oblong type glass containers on the handlebar of one's bike. The 'power' was discussed, at the turn of a knob one could hear music (vocal and instrumental), drama, and above all the weather forecast and the football matches. The older generation were derisory about the weather forecast. 'Did ye ever hear the like? That omadáun in 'the box' said the wind's from the west today and he forecast snow. All the world knows that if a horse or ass stands with his tail to the wind, we can expect bad weather. God blast the forecasters. It's a money makin' racket.' All 'the ramblers' veered towards the houses that had 'the box'. The 'Seanachies' hated the new contraption, they were ignored while the news and the weather were broadcast. "Mark my words, these new fangled ideas will bring misfortune down on us", they said. No wonder there's a war on when ye can't see who's spaking to ye. Ye should be able to argufy with people. It's not natural. Question Time was a popular radio programme. A team of interviewers went from town to town and asked questions from volunteer participants. The questions were simple and obvious - for example, 'How do you get down off a donkey?', answer, You can't – you can only get down off a goose. Another question was, name a county with a girls' name and an exclamation – "May O". Lord Haw Haw the Nazi propagandist radio presenter had an uncanny knack of finding out what was happening in Britain. He even knew details for instance that the clock in Rugby was five minutes slow. The good-night message on the radio suggested a peaceful and tranquil world, although the nations of Europe and especially Britain were suffering ruin and terror that was unprecedented by any standards. "Goodnight to all our listeners, whether they be on land, on sea, or in the sky . . . we wish you well . . . every hour of every day."

The emergency, as it was referred to in Eire, meant that most of the entertainment was manufactured by ourselves. The cinema, mainly makeshift ones in town and village halls, showed films that were vintage and outdated. They were mainly old Cowboy films; occasionally a romantic film was shown. They all seemed harmless, nevertheless they were heavily censored before they were released. Since it was dark in the cinema, the clergy decreed that all girls must sit on one side of the hall and boys on the other. To sit together was 'an occasion of sin'. It was difficult to make one's way down the aisle in the dark as the hands joined across the divide. I remember there was great jubilation in the clerical circles when the "Song of Bernadette", the film version of the story of St Bernadette of Lourdes, came to town. We were all encouraged to go, apparently it would improve "our souls". The older generation scorned 'the pictures' or 'pecthers' as they referred to them. However, The Song of Bernadette got such a glowing write up, especially from the pulpit, that an old, very pious couple decided that they must see it. If they were going into the war zone, there couldn't have been more preparations. The trap harness was polished until it shone, the trap itself was newly varnished, the pony was groomed and its mane plaited, it was like going to see de Valera all over again. The big night arrived, and Billy and Biddy walked into the cinema hall, bought their tickets, marched down to the front row and genuflected. They had difficulty with the tip up seats and complained that they couldn't kneel and pray before the performance. They talked about seeing "the Blessed Virgin" for years afterwards. The "Song of Bernadette" certainly made the cinema respectable, before this film the older people were doubtful about it but if it was good enough for Biddy and Billy, two pious saintly people, it was good enough for the likes of us.

The dance halls were the main form of entertainment for the youth. The halls replaced the house dances, which were very unpopular with the clergy. This always puzzled me. The house dances were a venue for all the generations and chaperoning would be comparatively easy. The hall dances were for the youth, they were held in new dance halls. The main ones in the Loughglynnn area were Gilligans in the village itself, the 'Memorial' in Lisacul, which was built in memory of the freedom fighter patriots who died for "the cause", and Gorthaganny and Fairymount in the outlying districts. The dance started about 9.00 – 10.00 p.m. and continued into the small hours. The entrance fee was generally a half a crown (26p in today's money). The walls in Gilligans hall were white-washed or painted with white emulsion. There were forms all around the walls where the girls sat or huddled together until they were asked to dance. The boys or bachelors congregated on the other side and eyed the girls up. They usually stood in groups, their main topic of conversation was 'the talent' or 'the mots', that's how they referred to the girls. The floor was wooden. In order to make it smoother for dancing, Lux soap flakes which had a shiny slippery consistency was scattered on the surface. There was a makeshift stage, where Teddy Macks band, later called "The Castlerea Dance Band" provided the music. I remember vividly my first dance. We had just received a parcel from my Aunt in Boston. It was the custom for relatives in the United States to send home parcels of used clothing to help out with the big families in the old country. The parcel contained a long flowery chiffon dress that must have been high fashion in the jolly nineties. It had a Victorian brooch to set it off. I thought it was marvellous. I had my first 'perm' the week before, and also my first pair of nylons; they were included in the America package. My ensemble caused great amusement in the family. Dad said, 'You look the spittin' image of your great Aunt B, she got married in a dress just like that'. My brothers said I looked like Dracula. My big sisters refused to go to the dance because I'd show them up. Mother, the peacemaker, said she'll have to learn. And I did. All the girls were in the makeshift cloakroom renewing their lipstick and titivating their hair when I arrived. They chatted with each other. An older group of girls in their late twenties or maybe thirties, eyed me curiously and remarked, 'aren't you too young to be out gallivanting?' I left the cloakroom with my friend and moved towards the forms by the tatty walls. The band was playing 'Give me five minutes more of your charms'. The hall was full of cigarette smoke and dust as the dance got into full swing. My friend was whisked away in the arms of the local Lothario. She was a magic dancer. I sat huddled against the greasy wall, ignored. I hummed the tunes under my breath – at least the band was good. The next dance was announced, 'Take your partners for an old time waltz'. My friend was talking animatedly to her dancing partner. He swept her on to the floor to the tune of 'I wonder who's kissing her now?' I waited, hope spring eternal I thought. Hope came in the shape of a middle aged bachelor shuffling towards me. He smelt of stale porter and pipe tobacco. It's ould Jimmy, I said, panicking, an' he's going to ask me to dance. And he did. I couldn't waltz, neither could he. You're Roger's girls aren't ye. I haven't seen ye here before, he said as an opening gambit. Will ye tell me now, how the blue springin heifer that I sould him at the fair in Ballagh is doin'? I don't know, I said. You must know if she's calved anyways. No reply from me, so he suddenly changed conversation tactics. 'That dress you're wearin' is just like the wan me mother had before she died, God rest her.' 'Amen' I murmured. I expect wan o' these days ye'll be on the look out for a farmer yerself. There's nothin' like a bit o' land an' a farmer's daughter makes a good farmer's wife. The hearth is empty now since the 'ould lady's gone, he said with a grin like an open steel trap that showed a mouthful of discoloured teeth like miniature tombstones. At desperation point, luck favoured me. The compére in shirt sleeves announced a 'lady's excuse me'. I spied a lad I knew from a neighbouring village, and almost sent ould Jimmy flying as I tore off to grab Mike and ask him to dance. Ye're in an awful rush Vera, I never knew you cared, said Mike teasingly. I glanced back at ould Jimmy, fearful that he might be in pursuit. Mike sized up the situation immediately. Has that ould codger been pesterin' you, he said. He's mad for a wife since his mother died. You could do worse, Vera, he said, teasing me again, he's got an ass, two cows and a brand new bike. He's been learning how to ride it for weeks. You can hear him up and down the boreen shouting out instructions to himself – "keep your feet on the paddles an' ye'er head straight". He's great gas altogether. WE both laughed, arrah, this ould hop is no good, said Mike. I borrowed the priest's bike to go to Lisacul but I changed me mind as it's a wild wet night. After this dance, jump on the cross bar an' I'll take you home. The cross bar, I said, will it hold me? It's a fine Raleigh bike with a dynamo lamp, he uses it for sick visits. Well, I said, my good spirits restored, make sure that you keep your feet on the paddles and your head straight an' we'll make it. Our laughter rang out in the young spring night as the March wind blew its shrill fanfare through the trees. My first dance wasn't so bad after all.

Rationing

"Will our bread supplies last until harvest? If everyone goes easy on bread; if everyone cuts down on wastage; if housewives are careful to make full use of all crusts, cold potatoes, left-over porridge etc, if we do these things, there will be no real shortage." Government notice – June 1941. Ration books were introduced by Mr Lemass in June 1942, although tea was rationed since 1941. The tea ration cards weren't very satisfactory, some shopkeepers refused to accept the cards, especially when the initial two ounces a week was halved, and later halved again. The rationing of tea was a great blow to the country people who invited you in for a cup o' char at any time of the day or night. It was a social occasion, a way of life which caused hardship when rationed. Our neighbour used to drop in on her way to the well. "Arrah isn't it takin' that ould kittle a long time to boil, I'm gasping for the tay." She'd then use her apron to boost the flames to hurry up 'the kittle' until the lid rattled. The standard test of pre-ration days 'tay' was thick and black and strong enough for a mouse to race across it. The tea pot was scalded then a fistful of tea would be put in the pot followed by boiling water. The tea pot would then be placed on cinders on the hob or the hearth to give it time 'to draw'. It was then poured into cups or mugs, sweetened with sugar and topped with cream from the crock. It was generally accompanied by soda bread spread with home made butter. It was a delicious mid-morning snack. My aunt was a semi-professional tea-leaf reader. Until the modern tea bags appeared, the genuine tea left a residue of leaves in the cup. My aunt claimed she could read 'your future' in the tea leaves. Usually after a dance the local girls would flock in to have their cups 'read'. It didn't matter if the sun was cracking the stones outside, the hay making would be abandoned while the cups were read. Of course my aunt knew all about the love-life of the colleens, and gave them a tremendous boost by re-assuring them that the tall dark handsome fellow that gave them 'a good show' at the dance had fallen head over heels in love with them, and there would shortly be wedding bells. The girls who had decided to emigrate (most of them had) would be told that 'they would cross the water and become immensely rich' or famous and marry money. This was a turnabout, as at that time 'dowries' or 'fortunes' were the norm if you married a farmer and stayed in Ireland. When rationing was introduced the tea drinking of necessity had to stop, and there was less excuse to drop in to neighbours. All sorts of advice was given to make the ration go farther. The papers advised that "a good substitute could be made for tea by a mixture of common ash and hawthorn leaves". Tea leaves were dried and used several times to try and re-create a strong brew, but all to no avail. It was weak and colourless, no substitute at all. Someone else suggested putting bread soda into the pot – this only turned the leaves white, but there was light at the end of the tunnel.

When the United States of America joined the allies, American troops referred to as GI's. were posted to Northern Ireland. A cousin of ours from Boston was posted to Derry city, and we were very excited when we received a letter to say that he and his friend would shortly pay us a flying visit. Immediately there was a great 'Spring Clean' organised. This was customary when the Yankee relations returned. The kitchen was white-washed, the neighbours came in to help. Patsy, a painter and decorator brought his paint and his glue-pot and painted the mantle-piece green. Al the Delft on the dresser was washed until it gleamed and shone. The chairs and 'forms' were scrubbed white, but the biggest job of all was erecting a closet, or toilet. All sorts of suggestions were put forward, eventually they decided on a corrugated iron structure with a white pail as the main appliance. I was given the job of cutting up the "Roscommon Herald" into squares, and putting a string through them for toilet paper, which was hung on the side by a nail. It took me hours. The toilet was greatly admired. It was placed discreetly at the end of the hay garden and the door was fastened with a big hasp. There was great excitement in the village when the two dashing Yankee soldiers arrived in a jeep. They were overwhelmed with the Cead Míle Fáilte. The partying started immediately. "Gee, it's just like Mom says Aunt Norah" said Steve. "There's no place in the world like Ireland an' no girl in the world like an Irish colleen". The girls all came to meet the GI's. My Aunt Maggie who was a magic concertina player, started off the music. She was joined by my friend Mary and our cousin John Dwyer, two great fiddlers, and an itinerant flute player by the name of Jack the Piper. I never did find out what his surname was. he must have been the last of the travelling music makers. The dancing began. The girls showed cousin Steve and his friend Warren, who he referred to as 'Buddy' how to dance a half set. The Yanks gave us a demonstration of a new American dance called the Hokey Cokey.

> Ya put your right foot in and your right foot out, You do the hokey cokey an' you shake it all about. You do the hokey cokey and you turn around,
> That's what it's all about.

Soon everyone joined in amid shrieks of laughter. Then the

singing began. "Musha Luke, ye'd have to give the Yankee lads a welcoming song to remind them of home, said Aunt Maggie. Luke was a bit shy at first but soon gave a fine rendition of "If the River Shannon flew through Boston City" followed by "If we only had old Ireland over here". Three local boys who had fine contralto voices sang the nostalgic ballad "Beautiful Loughglynnn" which was written by an Irish emigrant, a Miss Greevy from the Lisacul area.

> No artists' brush can paint her scenes
> Nor can a poet's pen
> That lovely lake, beyond my dreams
> called beautiful Loughglynnn.
> Tis there the swans glide gently on,
> the fish leap to the fly.

and

> I've seen the River Hudson, and the rocky shores of Maine,
> The beauty of Long Island, Connecticut's fair plain.
> But oft-times I am lonely and I'd like to take a spin
> and view the ideal of my dreams around my dear Loughglynnn.

They were wildly applauded. Mick Dwyer, a Mayo man, sang "Moonlight in Mayo". It was then time for 'the tay', but it was very scarce. The Yanks came to the rescue. "Say Buddy", said Steve, "we forgot to bring the presents from the jeep". They brought a huge cardboard box of goodies, cigarettes (which were very scarce), nylons for the colleens, white loaves, and the best of all, a box of tea bags. We all crowded round, it was like Aladdin's cave. My mother was anxious to know how to use the tea bags. The tea was in a flimsy tissue paper bag with a string attached. Buddy explained that you put it in a tea pot, poured scalding water in and let it brew. The string was left trailing on the saucer. The older people were delighted – lashings of real tay at last. What'll they think of next, aren't the Yanks great. What would we do without them. The colleens were overjoyed with the nylons and surreptitiously went into the low room to put them on. The GI's. noticed and told them they looked cute. The girls were very impressed with the dashing uniforms, the 'Clark Gable' 'taches and the jazzy jeep. The nylons helped as well. Steve requested one of Mom's favourite songs. "An we'll join the harp and shamrock with the star of liberty", as he winked at the prettiest girl in the house. As it was only a flying visit, the two young American soldiers left to the evergeen emigrant tune of 'Come back to Erin' and the shores of Amerikey. They promised to return, and with a cheery 'hats off to the Irish' and 'up Loughglynnn' they sped away to their base in Derry city. They were posted almost immediately to an American air force camp in Chorley, Lancashire. Warren was shot down in a raid over Berlin. Steve survived the war and returned to his native Boston. The day the Yanks came was a red letter day in our village, and was a talking point for a long time to come. "Tay bags – did ye ever hear the like, an' they made the finest mug o' tay ye ever tasted'. America is God's own country, said the delighted old folk.

Bread was also in very short supply. Wheat imports came to an end, and the Irish loaf consisted of 90 per cent wheat extraction. It was very healthy but very unappetising – you'd think it was made o' pig feed, or worse, the country people said. Cigarettes and tobacco were also virtually unobtainable. A popular hit song at the time was called 'You are my sunshine'. During 'the emergency' it went like this.

> You are my sunshine, a double Woodbine,
> a box of matches, a Craven 'A'.
> You never know dear how much I love you,
> so please don't take my sunshine away.

If you asked for cigarettes or tobacco, the shop-man would look through you and say icily No cigarettes yesterday, none today and none tomorrow, they're not makin' them any more'. But they were, you could get them at the 'black market' shop at £1 for ten Woodbines. Kerosene or lamp oil was also in extremely short supply. It was pre-rural electrification so country people had to depend on oil lamps for lighting. I remember learning my lessons by the light of the moon. Bicycles were the main mode of transport, but bicycle tyres, inner tubes and other essential bicycle parts were almost impossible to find. An improvised rubber tyre called a semi-solid bicycle tyre was manufactured out of old used car tyres. The car tyres were cut into semi-circular strips about 2" wide and glued together in the shape of a bicycle tyre. It felt as flat as a punctured inner tube, and was almost impossible to ride a bicycle with this disaster for a tyre. The innovation didn't last long. The immigrant workers used to smuggle tyres in from Britain, they used to fasten them round their waists as the exporting of rubber goods from war torn Britain was strictly forbidden and if the tyres were found they would be confiscated immediately by the Customs and Excise Inspectors.

THE EMERGENCY BOGEY-MEN

The Department of Agriculture issued a statement about the importance of self-sufficiency in food production. They emphasised the importance of making ourselves independent of imported food supplies. 'The drastic reduction in the importation of human and animal foodstuffs renders essential a greatly increased production of home grown food'. That is how some of 'the Emergency' bogey-men made their appearance, namely 'The Tillage Inspector' and 'The Warble Fly Inspector'. Everyone was urged to cultivate their gardens as well as the fields and compulsory tillage was imposed on the farming community. In theory this was a splendid idea, in practice it wasn't always easy to carry out. The tillage inspector had a habit of pouncing on his hapless victims, he would arrive with all the measuring paraphernalia that was required in order to ascertain if the prescribed amount of land was used for tillage. It was very difficult for older people and also for families whose main breadwinner, the father, had emigrated to Britain in order to make ends meet. Our friend and neighbour called Jamesy, or 'Mr M'Friend' lived in constant fear of a visit from the dreaded 'compulsory tillage man'. He could just about manage to till his garden. His chief topic of conversation was 'by Jingo, what if the quare fella comes to me'. The young lads who were always ready for a bit of excitement would embroider the supposed penalties exacted – a huge fine – maybe evict you, or worse still put you inside for a spell. Around this time my uncle Charlie from Galway, who had just retired paid us a visit. Jamesy was his boyhood friend. They all told him about the bogey-man tillage inspector, and how worried Jamesy was about his visit. I'll go to see him, said Charlie, an' give him a bit of a shock. Jamesy was making cart-wheels for his new cart when he spotted him. He dropped all his tools and limped towards him groaning loudly as if he had a severe attack of rheumatism. 'I've had the rheumatics for years sir - a neighbour has to help me to get in an' out o' bed, the pain is cruel and the doctor says he can do nothing for me. I'll be shoving up daisies soon an' that's the thruth sir. I'll never see another Spring'. Charlie could barely get a word in edgewise. Never mind your excuses, my good man, he said, come an' fetch me measuring chains in from me bike saddle. Ye're not goin' to measure me up are ye, said Jamesy as he hobbled after Charlie. Charlie opened the saddle bag and took out a half a dozen of Guinness. Jamesy couldn't believe his eyes. In his excitement he became straight as a ram-rod. You oul' fraud, said Charlie, don't you remember me? Well by jingo if it isn't our Charlie. I thought it was the quare fella, the tillage man. Jamesy didn't wait to shake hands but grabbed the Guinness, ran to the corner of the house, banged the neck of the bottle on the wall to open it (he never used a corkscrew), much too slow, and gleefully watched the black frothy Guinness pouring out. The two old friends collapsed laughing on the doorstep, supped their Guinness and talked about 'ould times'. The tillage inspector never did come to Jamesy, but he enjoyed telling the tale of how he thought Charlie was 'the quare fella', the compulsory tillage man who got paid to make life harder for people like himself. The warble fly-man's job was created in order to check that cattle which were infected by the warble fly were treated. Notices were posted in the Garda stations, post offices and other public places to remind people to 'get the warble fly – before it gets you or your live-stock'. The poster was quite frightening and was dominated by this life-sized mini-beast. The fly itself was a minute tick that embedded itself in the hides of cattle and caused diseases which stopped the beasts from thriving and eventually killed them.

They had to be examined every day, and if the fly appeared, treated with an antiseptic cocktail of Jeyes fluid, and other antiseptics. The warble fly inspector was a small gnome of a man with a shrivelled walnut complexion. He had enormous bulbous eyes like car headlights. When he popped up people used to say 'watch out, the warble fly is about'. The warble fly man was like a life sized version of the poster. Towards the end of the war all the inspectors who were generally despised, disappeared much to the delight of everyone.

EMIGRATION IN THE WAR YEARS

Emigration was a necessary evil during the war years. The economy was almost at a standstill, as it lacked the dynamism – participation in the war might have created. Farm prices plummeted, the farming community protested but there was nothing the government could do to alleviate the situation. In 1941 Sean Lemass froze incomes for the employed until the war was over. This was a harsh and bitter blow for the people who were lucky enough to have a job, but in the early to mid 1940s, 70,000 people were unemployed and the only solution for them was the emigrant ship. The fact that wages and salaries were frozen meant nothing to them as they had no jobs, and no prospects of ever finding one. Britain with all its man-power in the forces, was anxious for workers to man her industries. "The Irish government agreed with the British Ministry of Labour to ship us into exile", said an emigrant of the day. The cities' slums were badly hit, they were suffering extreme privation, so were the youth and the bread winners in the rural communities. In 1944 the Irish government gave £100,000 to alleviate distress in Italy. It was a deserving cause. At the same time the severe distress caused by massive unemployment at home was acute. I heard men who got short term employment in the turf cutting scheme complain that they were knee deep in water and their wellingtons or gum boots were worn to shreds and offered no protection. They were forced to mend them with bicycle tube patches and solution, that is if they could find it. The £100,000 certainly would have been put to good use at home. The price of rubber rocketed, the men and boys had to put up with wet feet. "There is nobody in this country who is not getting proper food" said de Valera at a meeting in Co. Clare in 1943. People with no income were poor because they had no jobs. The Bell stated that "malnutrition is prevalent all over the country", it also said that "TB and infant mortality was on the increase". Yet the 1937 Constitution said that "the State shall in particular, direct its policy towards securing that the citizens . . . may through their occupations find the means of making reasonable provision for their domestic needs". There was no 'reasonable provision' in sight so there was an exodus to war torn Britain of young people from every part of neutral Ireland. The government were delighted, because the exodus got them 'off the hook' as far as the embarrassment of massive unemployment was concerned. Emigrating to Britain during the emergency was quite complicated. Passports and identity cards were required and stamped with the motif 'Citizens of Ireland'. In order to protect the young emigrant men from being 'called up' for the British Army, de Valera signed an agreement with the British Ministry for Labour stating that if the men returned home after six months, they would be exempt from conscription. After a short break they could return to Britain and repeat the process. Big companies in Britain, for instance transport, hospitals, factories and personnel for military bases organised their own recruiting services. If one applied for a particular post, for instance nursing, the candidate would be informed by letter that a post was available, but they would not be told where the post was located. An interview would then take place in Dublin, and a group of girls would be told which hospitals they were accepted at, subject to health checks and other requirements. Most of the emigrants went to work in the ammunition factories. They had to go through a similar procedure, but they were given a label to wear which bore the logo 'British Factories'. They were herded together in tin roofed quayside sheds waiting for 'the boarding' to begin. When they reached their destinations the culture clash was immense. The barn-like massive munition factories with the incessant unrelenting noise, as well as the noise from overhead aircraft and the constant knife edge fear of air raids, was totally unnerving, especially for young people who were accustomed to wide open spaces and clean air. The money was fairly good, there was plenty of overtime and they could send remittances home; the living conditions were appalling. The land-ladies were having a field day, accommodation was very scarce, some of the traditional boarding houses in the inner cities were bombed, making bad matters worse. The landladies sorted out the problems by cramming as many beds as they could into one room, and by two or three people sharing one bed. The shift work system enabled them to have "double money" as when the night shift workers returned, they occupied the beds that the morning shift workers had vacated. The emigrants were exploited rotten and the only relief they had was to visit the pubs to get away from the misery of the boarding house. They organised Irish evenings in the pubs, and formed their own Ceilidh bands, which foreshadowed the later Irish centres, and thus instigated a resurgence of interest in Irish music and culture, which was almost moribund at the time. Some of the emigrants were very young, only sixteen to eighteen years old. There were no social workers, or religious organisations to monitor the conditions in which they lived, or to give the young people help or advice. It was to their credit and the credit of their parents that they adjusted so well to this alien environment. Many of them settled in Britain and contributed an enormous amount to the growth and economy of post-war Britain.

In the meantime they had to live through war torn Britain where air raids were the order of the day and night, where sirens sounded and bombers droned overhead. Hitler had conquered Europe, and the British Army was cut off along the French coast up to Dunkirk, where small boats ferried the soldiers back to Britain. The Germans now faced them menacingly across the channel, and Churchill made his famous speech:

> We shall defend our island home . . . if necessary alone . . . we shall fight on the beaches, we shall fight in the fields, and in the streets. We shall never surrender.

The real war had begun and the emigrants were in the middle of it. Many of them from Loughglynnn worked in the ammunition factories in the British Midlands, mainly Birmingham and

Coventry. These industrial cities were an obvious target for the Germans, and in 1940 the first bombers came to the Midlands. They came every night with monotonous regularity. A family of young men from Loughglynnn who worked in Coventry, described the carnage. "The sirens went early. It was a bright moonlight night on November 21st, we got a flask of tea ready, and prepared to go to the Anderson shelter for the night. It was a concentrated attack. The planes came over, dropping bombs - six in a row. We huddled under the stairs and table, we couldn't reach the shelter. The noise was deafening, it was an inferno, the whistling, the whooshing of the bombs grew louder and louder - and was accentuated by the crash of buildings that had received a direct hit. Our door was blown across the road, leaving a gaping hole where we had a grandstand view of the raging furnace which was once our street. We fully expected to be blown to Hell and kept counting each other for reassurance. The windows were shattered and there was a gaping hole in the roof where we could see cloud after cloud of red tearing through an angry sky. We were choking with the acrid dust and a sickly sulphurous smell of bombs. Searchlights criss-crossed crazily, and sirens vied with the bombs to create a veritable hell. We were too numb to pray or talk, and were amazed that we were all alive towards dawn, or we thought it was towards dawn. The sky was alight because Coventry was blazing. There was a lull, the bombs had stopped. We dragged ourselves up and stumbled along the red hot street. Our feet were scorched and blistered, we were hindered by fallen masonry and the gruesome sight of dead bodies and severed limbs. As we moved farther out of the city, we were joined by other stragglers, moving away in twos and threes like an army marching away from a lost battle. Some of them were carrying babies, a lot of them were bleeding and injured. When we reached the nearest village we were met by the Home Guard (later known as Dad's Army). They and other Church leaders took us to the village hall and plied us with food. They put us on a train to Stranraer where we caught a ferry for Larne, and home". Coventry, a great city, was bowed but unbroken. After the war Coventry Cathedral and Munster Cathedral in Germany were twinned. The communities from both cities met and made a peace compact, that never again would they engage in war. Part of the bombs that destroyed their Cathedrals can still be seen in Munster and Coventry.

The lot of the emigrant is a sad one. In the past at least as soon as they left the shores of Ireland they were, it seems, conveniently forgotten - marginalised. The exodus during 'the emergency' years illustrates the lowly status of the emigrants, who were given labels to wear to indicate their role in the workplace of the day. The fight for freedom didn't mean much to these young people, they were far too concerned about their future in a strange environment to bother about de Valera's dream. Not only did the young emigrants suffer the trauma of leaving home and adjusting to a new urban culture, there was a certain stigma attached to their leaving, the implied criticism was if they worked hard enough, and were patriotic enough, they could have stayed in their own country. Some of them did, they worked as domestic servants for a new elitist class for little remuneration. They became apprenticed to shop-keepers and served their time learning the trade of selling. They had to pay a fee for this privilege as well as working for no pay for three or four years for the employers. Eventually they joined the emigrant ship, to be further exploited or if they were lucky to make a good life for themselves in a foreign strand. Then there was the religious aspect. After all 'England wasn't Protestant any more, it was pagan', so the sanctimonious brigade who were pious and religious like the Taoiseach himself, watched closely to see if the exiles' faith was wavering. The answer to that, if they so chose, could be seen in all the Catholic churches in every corner of Britain. The churches were built with the pennies and pounds and the unstinting help of the exiles. These churches are a monument today to their devotion and loyalty to the Faith. Another favourite little conscience salving philosophy was that emigration was 'God's Will'. The young Irish were now spreading the gospel in foreign parts like the saints of old, and Ireland once again would be described as 'The island of Saints and Scholars' - all down to the misfortunate emigrants. Saints and scholars indeed – more like a new name for 'the Spalpeens'.

CHAPTER NINE
A JOB FOR ALL SEASONS

We children always had to write a composition or an essay in school each week, the seasons were a favourite topic. In fact we had to write two essays, one in Gaelic and one in English. I nearly always used Raftery's poem as an introduction to my composition on Spring, "Anois teact an Earrai béid an la dul cun sine". It had to be written in Gaelic script. Our teacher always described Spring as 'Seasun ná hoige', the season of the young - lambs, chicks, calves, birds, buds and shoots. Spring officially began in Ireland on February 2nd, St Brigid's feast day. On that day the restful Winter season ended, and no matter how cold or wintry the day was, people could be seen 'making a start' on the vegetable garden. This garden was a vital part of the family food economy. If the garden was dug early, it gave the earth a chance to renew itself, and make the soil porous and receptive to the young seeds and plants. In the Autumn the garden and the fields would be top-dressed or manured with natural manure in order to fertilise the land. There was little or no artificial manure, fertilisers or pesticides in the thirties in Ireland, and if there was, there was no money to buy them. All the farming therefore was organic and would be hailed today in our pesticide free farming methods with delight by the green organisation. The women were usually responsible for the kitchen garden. They also shared the work in the fields with their husbands and family. They often grumbled at the workload which included 'within and without'. All the family at an early age were incorporated in the running of the farm. Each member had a chore which they were expected to carry out, and were familiar with all the ins and outs of making ends meet in a small-holding. They were taught to be observant; for instance they would know when an animal was ready to give birth, or was 'in season'. There was no artificial insemination. The young folk automatically picked up all the crafts that were essential to survival on a small farm. These crafts were rarely taught formally, they were 'caught' or picked up by observing older people doing them. For instance, making a rick of turf was a work of art, it was the same principle as dry stone walling. The turf or sods had to be placed at the correct angle in order to protect the turf in winter from wind, rain and snow. It was referred to as 'freeing' and was a necessary addition to the winter haggard. The rich musky aroma of the ricks of hay and corn and the sharp tang of heather from the turf ricks, made the haggard a secure and fulfilling part of the small Irish homestead.

When the garden was ready and the days lengthened and got warmer, my mother would go to the Friday market in Ballagh and buy bundles of spring cabbage, which contained one hundred plants. There was different varieties of cabbage but "early York" was the most popular. By summer this cabbage plant which was miserable looking in early spring grew into large white heads and was delicious cooked with bacon, or bacon ribs. Alongside the cabbage plants were lorries of calves from Limerick. Local people were very suspicious of these healthy looking specimens because it was said that they were fed on buttermilk from the golden vale creameries and were susceptible to a disease called 'the white scour'. Cheek by jowl with the calves were crates of bonhams, who shrieked indignantly when farmers with their ash-plants came along and pushed and poked them through the crate in order to assess their worth. The plaintive lowing of the calves, the screeching of the bonhams, the strident voices of the 'Chape Jacks' with their colourful array of rags blowing in the wind, mingled with the good humoured heckling of the farmers' wives, made the square a lively and enjoyable scene. Market day was also a social occasion. Many a match was made in the square in Ballagh. It was an easy way to get an introduction to some 'eligible' male. All a girl on the look out of a husband had to do was ask the man she had her eye on to 'advise' her on the quality of the cabbage plants or the potential of the bonhams or calves. She couldn't be accused of being forward with this approach. When the ice was broken, a follow up was usually 'a treat' in Coleman's coffee shop, or a cosy drink in the snug in one of the many bars. It was less cumbersome, and less expensive than the old match-making method of 'drawing down' which involved stiff embarrassing meetings when both parties were asked by the match-maker if they liked each other. Even if they didn't, they had no alternative but to say yes, and both their futures were clinched, provided 'the fortune' and land aspect was also favourable. Coleman's bar and coffee shop was the most popular venue in Ballagh, especially for the country people. I used to hear the old ladies say that the late Mary Coleman made the first cup of coffee in Ballagh town, and it was the best you ever tasted, they said. She also had a glowing fire in the snug. When the country folk brought their American relations in to town for a treat, they always spoke highly of Mary's "cawfee". The Galway-Sligo bus also stopped at Colemans, and on market and fair days country people who cycled into town could return home by bus, as it had a roof rack which accommodated cycles and large parcels. The bus driver and his conductor were always very obliging and friendly. At Christmas time when people were buying Christmas things and were laden with brown paper parcels, they would cheerfully hoist them up on the roof rack, secure them with rope, cover them with tarpaulin and hand them down at the many stops on the route. At pig killing time, just before Christmas, I can still see the conductor climbing up the bus ladder at least five times with huge blocks of salt. On one dark evening the bus by-passed Shannons Cross where a farmer's wife should have alighted. She got very agitated as she had a block of salt on the roof rack. "How am I goin' to carry the salt back, with all me other parcels, an' worse still, me man's waitin' for it to salt the pig that was kilt the day before yesterday. It's hangin' on the back door, with an arran banner in its gob.

There'll be the mother an' father of a row if I don't get back with the salt quick". Don't worry ma'am, said the driver as he promptly turned the bus round at the school and took her back to Shannon's Cross. "God love ye", she said, "and may ye have a child every year". Don't pray for that missus, I have seven mouths to feed already". "The more the merrier" quipped the blacksmith, who was a regular passenger, and careless laughter rang out on the frosty star-filled night at Shannon's Cross.

When the garden was planted it was time for potato slitting, the seed potatoes were cut in order to make them go further. The potato cutter, or slitter (always the wife) had to make sure that the cut potatoes had 'eyes' for sprouting. It was a monotonous chore but it also had a social aspect. A group of women would meet in each other's kitchens and make short work of the chore. It was a great time for new or gossip, stories were whispered and embroidered in the telling – if you heard a bit of juicy news in the morning, you would hardly recognise it as night, so much would have been changed with colourful bits added on according to the whim of the story teller. I heard a farmer and a postman talking one day. "What's the quickest way to get news round these days, Bill" said the farmer. As quick a lightning the postman riposted, "telephone, telegram, tell a woman". Much of the talk was humorous and light-hearted. It was mainly about eccentric characters or the big nobs who had moved from the tuppeny class to the tuppence half-penny class and got above themselves. It wasn't all gossip and story telling. One of the women was a fine traditional singer, and in order to augment her repertoire of songs, she would bring along Old Moore's Almanac which printed ballads, old and new. All of them were very long. Once Biddy started with Old Moore's there was no stopping her. "We'll be here til Christmas at this rate" said a despairing wife, "she hasn't touched a pratie since she came in". "Arrah, never mind" said an old lady, "we have plenty o' time an' it's the first time I heard 'Bould Robert Emmett' sung through since I was a girleen". While the slitting was going on in the kitchen, the man of the house was usually out ploughing in the fields. Tractors were rare and pierce ploughs were fairly new as well. The plough was pulled by a team of farm horses and driven by two men, the farmer and a helper. Ploughing a field was an art in itself. For potato planting the ridges and furrows had to be straight and even. As the rich brown earth was turned over, one could scent the first hint of Spring in its loamy depth. Ploughing was hard physical work, with a slow measured pace which suggested timelessness. At the end of the headland the ploughman usually broke off for a smoke and a welcome swig of spring water soaked in oatmeal. The smoke was longed for and tobacco was often scarce. My father told me a story about a ploughman who ran short of tobacco and was desperate for a smoke. "Begob, I'd trade me horse there for a pipe o' baccy". Suddenly an ounce of 'plug' appeared on the grass. The ploughmen were jubilant and had their smoke. They had hardly finished when the horse dropped dead at their feet. The headland was partly a 'fairy fort'. After the ploughing came the planting of the potato seeds. A 'steveen' was used for this purpose, it was similar to a spade, but it had a pointed conical base. We children did the 'guggering' or putting in the seed potatoes. Good Friday was supposedly a very lucky day for sowing the new seed. After planting the potato crop was top dressed (manured) and moulded twice. In summer it was a welcome sight to see the green lush plants with the purple and white blossoms, a forerunner of the delicious 'cally' or colcannon to come. It was now time to spray the crop to prevent it from being blighted. This was an important and essential part of the successful growing of the crop, as echoes of the famine blight still rankled in the minds of the people. Spraying was a messy job. A barrel of water with about 14 to 16 lbs of bluestone diluted in it and steeped overnight was placed at the edge of the potato field. The sprayer had to cover himself in hessian bags as the spray was lethal. The spraying machine which was made of copper and was fitted with a flexible hose held about 2 gallons of deep blue spray and was attached to the back of the sprayer. The solution was sprayed on to the flowering stalks and prevented the dreaded blight.

Cutting and rearing the turf was an important item in the late spring agenda. The blazing turf fire which traditionally was never extinguished was the heart of the home. When the dispossessed famine families had to flee to the coffin ships, they took with them a sod of turf to bring them luck and to remind them of their lost heritage. Turf cutting was an arduous task. First of all the bank was cleared. This involved clearing scraws and scrubs from the surface. When the bank was cleaned, a slane was used to cut into the first spit, 'a spreader' in the hollow with a wheelbarrow would catch the wet spongy sods of turf and dump them in a heap, later to be scattered and footed into 'groigins' and when dry, clamped. This process could only be done satisfactorily if the weather was good. Days on the bog were semi-social occasions, all the families had bogs adjoining each other, they told jokes and stories and sang songs as the larks rose from the heather and soared trilling into the sky, while the snipe and other bogland creatures ran for cover at the rude intrusion of their habitat. Dinner time was the highlight of a day in the bog. We children would light a fire to boil a black bog kettle for the longed for tea. Sometimes we'd roast potatoes on the fire but mostly we'd eat boiled bacon and brawn sandwiches. Families from neighbouring bogs joined us, told stories and had a singsong. The scalding tea, mingled with the heathery smoke of the fire, the bogland breeze which blew through the waste land of young gorse heather and ceannawans, the trilling of the lark and the laughter of the people made working on the bog a joyous time. In late summer the turf was carted home and stacked in a rick in the garden. A cosy winter kitchen with a roaring fire could be looked forward to.

Hay cutting time started in late June or early July; this coincided with the school holidays. Again it was the days before the farm horse was replaced by the tractor. The mowing machine pulled by a team of horses could be handled by one man. The weather was all important in the hay-making season. I remember my father and his friends anxiously looking at the weather – local weather beliefs were taken very seriously. A red sky at night was a good sign, a ring round the moon was ominous. When the first radios appeared, farmers used to listen anxiously to the man in 'the box' for the weather report. If the weather turned nasty, he got all the flak. "Did ye hear what that eajit in the box said, the weather is set fair, and look at it rainin' cats and dogs". Without fine weather the ripe meadow couldn't be tackled. It needed the sun to dry the early morning dew off the grass before cutting. Looking back on those far off summers of my youth, the sun seemed to be always shining. When the summer holidays began, for two or three weeks the village would be heavy with the fragrant heady smell of new mown grass. The whole place was dominated by hay, it was a major topic of conversation. It was everywhere, the roadside hedges were festooned with it as it mingled with the wild rose and wild woodbine. All the hay-making was done by hand using long wooden rakes and two pronged hay forks which had to be handled with care. The rake was easy to handle, but I still remember the painful blisters after a day's work. When the hay was but into swarths, it was allowed to dry a little and was then turned with a rake and made into 'windrows' and then 'lapped'. Finally the laps were scattered into 'beds' and made into small cocks. The cocks were secured with ropes made out of hay. I always thought this was a magic process. I remember holding a stick horizontally in my hands while my father deftly fashioned a rope from the newly saved hay, as I moved backwards winding the stick faster and faster, as the hay rope grew longer and longer. In the afternoon jugs or sweet cans of tea and piles of newly baked soda bread with lashings of butter were brought to the hay field by my mother. We all sat on the new saved or half saved hay and drank tea from enamel mugs. It was a delightful soothing, never to be forgotten, part of my childhood in Loughglynnn. Bringing in the hay was a day for work and celebration. A 'mehill' was usually organised. The 'mehill' system dated back to pre-famine days, it was a system of cooperative seasonal farm work. For example, when a farmer was ready to bring in the hay, his neighbours would arrive on the appointed day. They were never given money as a reward, but there would be a lavish spread of food, drink, and in the evening a harvest ceilidh. They would also be given an assurance that their help would be reciprocated. Some of the 'mehill' made the hayrick in the garden while other groups brought the hay cocks in from the fields on farm carts. Another method of bringing home the hay was called 'snigging'. Traces or chains were fastened around a cock of hay, and a pony happily dragged it along the meadow to the haggard. The hay cock left a silvery path in its wake. As the pony set off with the cock (led by a man or boy) we children would gleefully jump on to the hay cock, snuggle into its sweet depth as it spread a summery fragrance around, and enjoy a glorious ride. Occasionally, if the pony galloped, we'd slide on to the fresh green after grass, only to jump on again as soon as we caught up. At dinner time, the mehill all filed into the kitchen for a scrumptious dinner of home cured bacon, early York white cabbage and a big Victorian dinner plate of floury potatoes. Across the years I can still see these men, our neighbours, sitting at the table with their caps on their knees, peeling the steaming potatoes and putting the world to rights with their tales and lore. In the evening the music makers made their way to the house and the harvest hooley ended a memorable day.

CHRISTMAS IN LOUGHGLYNNN

Christmas was a magic time in my childhood years. We saved our pennies up for months to buy simple presents. Christmas began for us when our parents went on the horse and cart to the local shop for 'the Christmas things'. By today's standards the Christmas fare was very basic; sultanas, currants, orange peel, caraway seeds, custard powder and jelly and a huge bottle of H.P. sauce formed the bulk of the Christmas commodities, and were a treat. We had our own Christmas dinner in the shape of a fat goose who was given extra special supplies of grain to make her taste good and juicy. I remember my mother used to make sloe and elderberry wine for a Christmas treat. A little of this wine was very good for us, according to my mother, as the fruit came straight from the hedgerows. We kids decided that if it was good for us, it would also benefit the goose, so we filled a small drinking trough with the wine and of course the goose got tiddly. She was falling all over the place. My mother was very anxious, she must have caught some disease. She dosed her and locked her in the hen house for a day and the next day she was as sprightly as ever, much to everyone's relief, especially ours. Out Christmas dinner was assured. My mother killed and plucked the goose two days before Christmas. She would then suspend it from a hook on the ceiling and prepared it for the oven on Christmas eve in readiness for dinner on Christmas day. It was a delicious meal. The oven was lightly greased and placed on hot cinders, the prepared and stuffed goose was placed in the oven covered with strips of home cured bacon and surrounded by pork sausages. The stuffing was an amalgam of bread crumbs, sultanas, mince-meat and aromatic herbs. The aroma was mouth watering. The roast goose, when cooked, was placed on a large brown willow patterned meat dish and put in the centre of the kitchen table, flanked by a bottle of H.P. sauce. For us children, the sauce was the epitome of culinary sophistication. When our teacher asked us at school what our favourite Christmas dinner was, I proudly said "roast goose and H.P. sauce". The main course was followed by apple pie and custard, and a small glass of elderberry wine. My mother was a wonderful baker. She specialised in making yeast bread. She used to have difficulty in obtaining yeast as it was used in the distilling of poteen which was illegal, but she always used to find some for her yeast bread. The dough when mixed and kneaded was placed in a big crock, covered in white muslin and put next to the fire to rise. It was fascinating to watch this process. When completely risen it appeared above the rim of the crock. It was then re-kneaded, decorated with strands of yeast dough, glazed with egg white and baked. I have never tasted bread as delicious as my mother's home made yeast bread. Her Christmas gifts to her friends and neighbours was always the celebrated 'Nora's East bread'. Our Christmas evening treat was gingerbread, currant, raisin and caraway cake and jelly. We made the jelly in two pound jam jars. I can still see them in a gleaming row on the dresser, full of bright green and red wobbly jelly. We also devoured the oranges and apples which "Santy" put in our Christmas stockings on Christmas Eve.

On Christmas Eve we decorated the house with holly and ivy. Berried holly was very sought after but usually it could only be found in the depths of Sabbath wood or in "the laurels". We gathered pine branches from "the clump" which was resinous and aromatic and brought the outdoors into the house. Except for a few coloured balloons there were no glitzy decorations. When darkness came my mother put a single lighted candle in each window – this was a tradition to welcome any travellers who passed that way, particularly homeless people. It was said that the Christ-child Himself at one time visited an Irish home disguised as a beggar. Towards midnight the Christmas bells rang out as we all trooped to Midnight Mass in the Convent Chapel. The walk to Mass along the ryde and avenue was thrilling as the ground was usually covered with hoar frost or light snowflakes. We children broke the frost on the puddles with our heels, which reflected the splintered star light. Midnight Mass in the Convent Chapel in Loughglynn was, and is, my idea of Heaven as the nuns sang "Venite Adoremus" like choirs of angels and we all gathered around the crib to celebrate the birth of Christ. It was a fitting start to the wonderful feast of Christmas.

On St Stephen's day, now referred to as Boxing day, we all decked ourselves out in fancy dress, (generally the head gear was feathers plucked from the wing of the goose, and painted) and took our flutes and musical instruments around the neighbourhood and entertained them with songs and music. Our introductory rhyme was "Up with the kettle and down with the pan, give us a penny to bury the wran" (wren). This would be followed by a request of the people in the house that we visited to sing a song of their choice. I remember we nearly always sang our very own national anthem, "The woodlands of Loughglynn", a great song for a great village, and a fitting way to end the magic of Christmas in the Loughglynn of my childhood.

CHAPTER TEN
"BURY ME DACINT'

Births, marriages and deaths were part and parcel of everyday life in my youth. They were a major topic of conversation, although old style matchmaking was on the wane. The 'fortune or dowry' culture however was alive and kicking, and marriages were still arranged. There weren't many 'love' matches, and if there were the couple emigrated and made a life for themselves in the country of their adoption. The 'farm' was inherited by the eldest son. The rest of the family emigrated; if they had relatives in America they were usually 'taken out' by them. This meant that their passage was paid. It was understood however that their passage money would be repaid as soon as the emigrant got work. Work for my mother's generation of women meant domestic services in the mansions of America's affluent society. The girls started off as junior housemaids, or "tweenies" and progressed through the culinary ranks to cook-housekeeper. They always sent remittances home, and when and if they returned for a visit, they were immediately dubbed 'the Yanks'. Not only did they lose their homeland and family but also their identity. Occasionally they stayed home and married a local farmer. They were greatly in demand on the marriage market as everyone assumed they were "rotten with money". In my youth, farmers married very late in life. The reason for this was that generally they shared the farmhouse with their parents, and the mother was accustomed to being 'boss'. The parents also expected a fortune from their son's bride. I heard the older people talking about a wedding that took place in the vicinity. After the wedding the bridegroom bade 'good-bye' to his new wife at the church door. "The ould lady tould me to tell ye, that she won't let ye put a foot inside the door, unless you pay her the £100 that was promised when the match was made", he said. The girl went home, bought a pair of bonhams in Ballagh, fattened them up, sold them, and continued to do this until she made up the fortune money. She gave the £100 to her mother in law, who promptly gave it to her daughter for her dowry. So the marriage 'merry-go-round' went on. Another marriage trick in an earlier era was to include a neighbour's field or stock in the prospective bridegroom's assets in order to impress his future in-laws, and also to enhance the fortune. Worse than that was the skulduggery that went on occasionally, when the prospective couple met and were asked if they 'liked each other'. It was said that an old farmer, anxious to get a not so young, unattractive daughter off his hands, sent a younger prettier daughter to meet the prospective groom in her place. The groom was delighted and boasted that not only was he getting a big fortune with his môt, but 'a great looker' as well. Pride comes before a fall; when he met his bride at the altar he couldn't believe his eyes, "she had a face that the divil designed". He realised he was hoodwinked, and when the priest asked him "will you take this woman to be your lawful wedded wife", he said "I'd see her in Hell first" – promptly turned on his heel in front of the crowded congregation, got on the train to Galway and headed for America. Mothers of marriageable sons had a very sceptical view about beauty, and good looks as requisites for a future daughter-in-law. A slick matchmaker was anxious to 'make a match' with an affluent farmer. He had to win the mother's approval. She's the loveliest girl ye ever laid your eyes on, he said to the future mother in law. In fact she's a beauty. Arrah, beauty never biled the pot Mick, said the ould lady. An it never stopped it from bilin ayther, said the exasperated match-maker. The 'made' matches seemed to work reasonably well, land not romance was at the heart of the rural marriage. The couple, and later the children had a common bond between them, feeding the calves, milking the cows, doing the never ending seasonal work ensured that they were always busy. In an era when there were no hand-outs, keeping the wolf from the door was a full time occupation.

Marriage however wasn't all moonlight and roses. One old couple were for ever daggers drawn. The wife, a big blowsy woman, had an awful tongue. Her husband was a mild little man who was often on the receiving end of the tongue lashing. Eventually the worm turned. "I'll tell the priest about ye when I go to confession on Saturday", he said. "Ye can tell the Pope if you like", she retorted, "you good for nothing latchikoe". He went to confession and poured out a litany of grievances to the priest. "Hell won't be full till she's in it Father". "Do you have sexual relations" said the priest when he got a word in edgeways. "We have no relations be that name Father, I cam to tell ye about me bugger of a wife, not about me relations", he said indignantly. He told the story to the neighbours, much to their delight. "Wasn't that a quare question to ask ye" said one sly old fella, "did ye tell 'herself'?" "I will wan day soon, but not yet" said Barney. So the arranged marriages had their ups and their downs. The dating agencies of today are a more sophisticated version of the match-making of yester-year. As the custom was dying out a farmer put an advertisement in Ireland's Own for a wife. "Wanted: Wife with tractor, write to this address and send photo of tractor".

A TIME TO BE BORN AND A TIME TO DIE

Births were generally enthused over, families were big and a regular addition was the norm. If a prospective bride was suspected of misdoing before she married, she was observed very closely, dates were kept and if a baby arrived before the allotted time it was a cause for gossip and whispered innuendoes. "Sure the child was a seven month birth, ye understand, but it was a fine bouncing baby all the same". "Troth, she's only been married six months according to my reckoning". "She was lucky he wed her in the nick o' time, sure the weddin' an the christening were nearly together". Woe betide any girl who had the misfortune to get pregnant outside the holy bonds of wedlock. Both she and her family were shunned, she was treated as a social pariah and usually ended up in a Magdalen home for 'fallen women". It always amazed me that the man concerned got off scot free. Today's society has a more Christian outlook. A notice in an Irish post office drew attention to additional entitlements for single mothers. A far cry from the pitiless attitudes to single mothers in my youth.

'Churching' was an archaic religious custom that was handed down from the mists of time. After a woman gave birth she was obliged to be "churched" by a priest. It was a form of purification service which allowed the new mother to return to the fold fully cleansed and shriven. This quaint ritual emphasised the obsession with sin which was prevalent at the time.

In my childhood and in my youth I never recall the doctor visiting us. We survived the measles, the whooping cough and the flu without any repercussions. Diphtheria and scarlet fever were raging at the time and the government initiated an inoculation jab to prevent infection. I remember filing up in twos from school to Dr Kelly's dispensary in order to be vaccinated. We had to roll our sleeves up, the doctor gave us the injection, dabbed the spot with iodine and we all trooped back to school and continued with our sums and writing. An old lady that I knew was one day stricken with severe chest pains. Her daughter who was home from America called the doctor behind her back. When he arrived, the old lady was furious. He examined her and said "I think it's your lungs, Sara". She was recovering by this time as she had a few nips of brandy before he arrived. "Me lungs is it doctor?" she said. "Well listen to me now, when we had nayther lungs, liver or heart, there was niver a bother on us. You've put me in a fix doctor, all the neighbours will think I'm dyin', an I intend to live till I'm a hundred". Sara was right, the signal for a death and the inevitable corpse house and wake was "Did he hear that ould Jamie, or Biddy had the priest and the doctor". The priest generally came first, and as sure as night followed day, the old person would die within a day or three of having "the priest and the doctor". It was a traumatic time for the bereaved household. The old people were respected and were generally treated with affection. Their main worry was not as in today's society, the fear of ending up in an old people's home which have been described as 'waiting rooms for the cemetery', but the fear that they wouldn't be given a decent burial. 'Bury me dacint' was the cry of the elderly. They penny-pinched, they took out small insurance policies, put their meagre savings in a bag under the mattress so they could have this lavish send off to impress their friends and neighbours in a dignified departure. It was a hectic time for the bereaved household. The corpse had to be 'laid out'. A group of women generally performed this very difficult and sensitive final service. This entailed washing the corpse and clothing it in a brown habit. The 'remains' were then reverently placed on the death bed, with the rosary entwined in their fingers, a crucifix at the head and lighted blessed candles on each side of the bed. The water in which the corpse was washed was called 'suff', thus the expression 'suff on you' was a curse of the greatest malevolence, indicating that they wished the accursed person dead. When the corpse was finally laid out, sympathisers flocked in to the 'corpse house'. They knelt and prayed by the bed-side, and then sympathised with the bereaved family. "I'm sorry for your trouble" was the stock phrase of condolence, followed by a paean of praise for the deceased. "He was a grand man, an' a great neighbour, he never did any harm to anyone, he wouldn't hurt a fly". In the Irish 'corpse house' "the good that men did lived after them, the evil was oft interred with their bones" until after the funeral and the wake at any rate. Light refreshments were given at the corpse house. The wake was held at night and lasted until the next morning. If the deceased was old, the wake was a jolly occasion, the dead man or woman was talked about in glowing terms - which improved during the night as the whiskey flowed. Clay pipes and pipe tobacco were handed round and a barrel of porter was set up in the farmyard. A lavish spread of food was set out in the high room or parlour and everyone was invited to the wake supper. Occasionally weeping or keening women would start up an eerie lament, but this custom was dying out in my time. Ghost story telling and anecdotes in connection with the deceased was the main entertainment. Neighbours acted as grave diggers. The corpse would be taken to the church on the evening after the wake and on the following morning a high funeral Mass would be offered for the repose of his soul, followed by burial at the cemetery. The mass and funerals were closely monitored, as the numbers at the mass, funerals and internment, was an indication of the respect accorded to the deceased and his family. Cars were counted, heads were counted, the elite were counted. "Did ye ever see such a fine funeral, if only ould Jamie, or whoever the deceased was, could only see it, wouldn't he be the proud man. Sure he'll be on the right hand side of "the man above" anyways, an' he'll see it all. Then inevitably came the sting in the tale; but did he deserve it . . . after . . . and then a whispered detrimental innuendo, an' do ye think that ould T.D. in his motor car would come, only for he's after the votes. Ye're right there, only for that he wouldn't be seen dead at ould Jamie's funeral – God rest his sowl.

In modern Ireland's money based 'tiger economy' the traditional burial customs are rapidly disappearing. Bereaved families do not as a rule "wake" their dead. Discreet chapels of rest are springing up like mushrooms in nearly all the towns, and the deceased is taken there prior to interment. After the burial, family and friends are invited to a meal in one of the posh hotels. I was asked to one of these dinners recently. My mind wandered back to an old wake of my childhood when I listened enraptured to the story-teller's tales. As I ran home fearful through the moonlit wood, I kept imagining that the tall trees were ghosts, and the eerie sounds of the night owls were Jamesey's friends welcoming him to his new abode. My heart nearly stopped when Jamesey's old black ass popped out from behind a tree braying loudly. I could have sworn the dark shadow behind the tree was Jamesy himself. It was a great relief when I fell in to our lamp-lit kitchen. My mother said "you look as if you've seen a ghost". "I think I have" I said, and breathlessly told my tale. "Don't worry" said mother, "the dead never come back, they're too happy in heaven". "Don't you believe her" said Dad, "they haunt you for ever if you don't 'bury them dacint'."

CHAPTER ELEVEN

ECHOES OF LOUGHGLYNN

THE LOUGHGLYNN DRAMATIC SOCIETY
Entertainment in my youth had of necessity to be organised by the people themselves. Dramatic societies mushroomed and Loughglynn drama society was second to none. Occasionally they used Gilligan's hall in Loughglynn for their performances but the main event of the year was held at the Convent hall. Both halls have been demolished. The Convent hall was not an integral part of the mansion but was tagged on to the main building. It was constructed of heavy duty zinc. The seating accommodation in the front rows were easy chairs. The Canon had a comfortable arm-chair all to himself, and was flanked by all the local 'aristocracy'. The middle area had chairs, and the back of the hall had long forms. The ticket prices reflected the seating arrangements as well as the social status of the audience. Tickets were 2/6 (12.5 pence) for the two front rows, 2/- (10 pence) for the next tier and 1/- (5 pence) for the rear forms. As far as we were concerned it was equivalent to the Abbey or any of the other great theatres of the day. I can still see the beautiful hand painted back drop on the stage, of moonlight shining through trees, and reflected on water. The stage was also cleverly contrived to accommodate other scenes appropriate to the programmes which were on offer. The late Nan Freeman who was a competent pianist made the rafters ring with her wide repertoire

of popular music which entertained us before the main concert began. This was a jolly prelude to the main performance and put us all in a festive mood for the enjoyment to come. The concert was a variety performance but the core of the entertainment was the play, usually produced and acted by the Loughglynn Dramatic Society. The members of the drama group were the late George Reid and Billy Hester, also the late Mary Kate Harrington and Rose Ann Crawley. Happily many of the performers are still with us, including Alex Reid, Jim Harrington and Chap Timothy. Match-making was a favourite theme for the plays, and usually Mary Kate Harrington lost her man to the glamorous Rose Crawley, (both girls were glamorous in real life). I'll always remember Mary Kate's plaintive resigned voice saying "Tis better to have loved and lost than never to have loved at all". Another play that I vividly remember was Lady Gregory's 'The Rising of the Moon'. As we didn't have any access to other live performances, these amateur productions were enjoyable and stimulating. The singing, the recitations, the music makers and the dancers made very lively entertainment. The highlight of the evening was the young singing priest - the late Revd. Martin Reid, who was of professionally singer status. His rendering of Padraic Column's haunting melody 'She moved through the Fair' was sheer delight to listen to, and held us all spellbound. Visitors to the Convent showed a great interest in the annual concert. One very distinguished visitor, the actress Barbara Mullen took part in one St Patrick's Day performance. She gave us a short humorous account of her early life in America where she told us she belonged to 'the poor Irish' before she joined her father Patrick Mullen in the Aran Islands She then gave a recitation entitled 'Pegeen Kelly's black cat', after which she danced an Irish jig. She said dancing was her first love, but emphasised that laughter and good humour were vital assets for a happy and stable life. In later years Barbara Mullen starred in many notable BBC television programmes, the most famous being Dr Finlay's Casebook where she portrayed a Scottish housekeeper. Another memorable character in the Convent hall productions was Ben Connolly who had a business in Loughglynn and who acted as compére at all the concerts. His announcements prefaced by, "Reverend Fathers, Reverend Mothers, Reverend Sisters, ladies and Gentlemen, the next item on tonight's star-studded programme is . . ." He would then continue to give a graphic description larded with humour and vastly exaggerated of the item which was to follow. Ben's announcements were as entertaining and dramatic as the items themselves. At Christmas time there was usually a nativity play where local children performed. They were nearly always on their best behaviour, the Angels looked as if they had dropped straight out of Heaven, but one Christmas St Joseph failed to appear and Mary got very agitated. She forgot her holy demeanour - hands joined, head bowed, she jumped up and with arms akimbo, lapsed into the local vernacular and in a very un-Mary-like way demanded of the angels "Where's himself gone, will ye tell me". The angels giggled and chorused, "he's gone to the closet", an old name for the toilet or lavatory. As Joseph sidled in sheepishly, Mary berated him. "Where wor ye, ye eegit, laven' me with the child in the cradle". The nuns were aghast, but the audience applauded loudly. This was surely more like Nazareth where the Mother of God and St Joseph had normal little problems like ourselves. It couldn't have been all angels and heavenly music in the chilly stable, so Mary brought a homely touch with her little outburst. The concert usually ended with 'The Holy City' and the National Anthem. By today's standards the concert in the Convent hall was a first class performance. The hall is now demolished and when I see the tarmacadammed space where it stood, I recall the friends of my youth, the music-makers, the artistes, the dancers and the singers, whose melodies linger on and are evocative of a more leisurely and carefree era.

THE CORPUS CHRISTI PROCESSION

The annual Corpus Christi procession which took place in the convent grounds was a religious but also a semi-social occasion. It started at the church after second mass on the feast of Corpus Christi. The people congregated outside and there was great huffing and puffing and ordering, as the different pillars of the church, the Men's Sodality, the Women's Sodality, the Children of Mary, the choir and the choir-mistress organised themselves for the procession. The Men's Sodality carried a banner depicting the Sacred heart, and the Women's Sodality carried one depicting the Virgin Mary. Of course, most of the congregation were on-lookers, they were happy to pray - and watch, and say how it should be done. On one occasion the elegant lady bearer of the Virgin banner got it in a twist, dropped it, and it landed on a cow pat. Look at her, as proud as a paycock, said an onlooker, an' she's after makin' a divil of the Blessed Virgin. She's got it comin' to her, they said gleefully as she tried to retrieve her dignity, much to the amusement of the crowd. The Children of Mary were the cynosure of all eyes, dressed in their sky blue mantles and carrying a banner saying 'A Child of Mary will never perish'. I'll have to join them, said a wrinkled old hag, I don't know about you Lizzie, but I'm perished with the cowld. You'll be even coulder if you join that lot, said Liz, they spend every Sunday in the chapel, and it's 'thou shalt not do this, and thou shalt not do that' an' if they as much as look at a lad, it's God help them. The 'ould maids' spy on them, any road they won't get kicked out, they're on the shelf an' there's no wan to dust them. Divil mend them. Tell me, is that Julia over there in the green silk dress an' the big hat with the feather. She looks like Lady Muck an' no mistake. Arrah, fine feathers make fine birds Liz. I'll put me specs on, said Liz. Troth, you're right, tis her – an look at the long ear rings jangling and dangling. She must have got a parcel from the Yanks. Wherever she got it, she looks like an ould Christmas tree tarted up. It's far from earrings, she was raired with her 'bageen' apron an' her two left clogs. The Christian conversation was interrupted by the sound of marching feet and an occasional drum beat. Begob, if it isn't the new Irish army, the local defence force, said Mike, an old soldier who fought on Flanders fields. You could see the glint of battle in his eye as the new army marched up. Ould Miko was soon joined by the other battle scarred veterans of all the wars fought on and off Irish soil. The Local Defence Force, or the L.D.F. was initiated by the government during 'the Emergency' to defend us from possible invaders. They'd put 'Dad's Army' in the shade with all the drillin' and marchin' and the hierarchical ranks - starting at Captain, there was terrible wrangling and jealousy with the ranks over these titles. 'Will ye look at them' said an old freedom fighter, 'they have no privates, did ye ever see the likes o' that, an army with no privates. All Chiefs and no Indians'. 'LEFT, RIGHT, LEFT RIGHT. Right turn', said the captain as they were leading the procession. He himself promptly turned left and put the whole proceedings into disarray. 'Will ye look at them – right "latchikoes" they'd be blown to hell in Flanders.' Ye're right there Miko, they don't know their arse from their elbow. They don't hould a candle to our lads here ayther, said an old revolutionary. Can ye see them licking the tans? The parish priest and his entourage – the curate and the altar boys all dressed in full canonicals, were getting restive. Make up your mind Captain, are we going right or left, said the Canon. He was not amused. This is a spiritual occasion brethren, he intoned, as he glared at ould Miko and his buddies. Arrah, why doesn't he sprinkle a dropeen of holy water over the captain to put him right, whispered Miko. An' he could bless them - the poor misfortunate eejits. You have no room to talk Miko, you took the saxon shilling and fought on Flanders field. An' where wor you when the fightin' was goin' on here - under the bed, that's where. The choir mistress and choir were getting hoarse singing 'Faith of our Fathers' and 'O Mother I could weep for mirth', which was very apt,, if they left out the mirth. They were saving the benediction hymns 'Adoremus', 'Tantum Ergo' and 'O Salutaris' for the three benedictions celebrated in the convent grounds.

Eventually the captain got his army organised and we all processed with a hymn and a prayer from the Canon, interspersed by the whispers, innuendoes and good natured banter from the female congregation.

On reaching the convent, Benediction was held in the magnificent little chapel. After Benediction the Canon carried the monstrance to the hall door where four of 'the nuns men' were waiting with a canopy to protect and honour The Blessed Sacrament and the Canon bearing it reverently. The priest was flanked by altar boys, holding lighted candles and looking like cherubs in their black and white soutanes. A group of first communicant girls all dressed in white walked backwards and strewed flower petals in front of the Blessed Sacrament. Weeks before our favourite phrase was "we're stewing in the procession". The Reverend Mother and the Franciscan Community, all clad in white habits of St Francis were next, they were followed by the lay sisters and last the young demure postulants and aspirants who were on probation before they were accepted into the novitiate, in order to train for missionary work in every part of the globe. Looking back over the years the Corpus Christi procession was a simple profession of faith where we all gathered to pray and to laugh. It was enhanced by the backdrop of the elegant mansion and the magnificent well kept grounds. The heady scent of the roses mingled with the new mown grass, and the bird song from the laurels and woodlands accompanied the singers. The final Benediction was celebrated at the front door of the convent facing the lake, where the stately swans glided gently along – and the ancient beeches stooped to kiss the wavelets as they lapped unceasingly on the sandy shore.

The convent is now a nursing home for elderly ladies. The beautiful little convent chapel is now a dining room. A modern church has been built in its place. The young postulants and aspirants of my youth have come back to the peace of Loughglynn after travelling all over the world to give succour to the sick, the maimed, the outcasts, the lonely and the dying. They no longer wear the beautiful cream habit of St Francis – most of them wear secular dress. All of them whom I spoke to could write a best seller about their extraordinary adventures, courage and selflessness against tremendous odds in the tropics. One sister told me a story about her time in Liberia. The Bishop visited the convent and the Reverend Mother decided for protocol's sake to invite the Chief of the tribe as well. After dinner all the sisters filed in and kissed the Bishop's ring. The Chief said, Bishop I am very impressed with how docile your wives are, I would like you to tell me how you do it. Sadly there are no young postulants today in the convent at Loughglynn – hopefully the Franciscan Missionaries of Mary, who made such a tremendous contribution to Loughglynn will remain as our neighbours, we have great affection and respect for the

Franciscan sisters. Why do good looking girls want to join the convent, said the old men, when the nuns first came to Loughglynn. The answer was given to me very recently by a Franciscan sister who has travelled the globe helping the sick, the maimed, the downtrodden and the outcasts, and who still works with them in the inner city of Chicago. She simply said, 'We were called and we answered'.

THE TRAVELLERS (GYPSIES AND TINKERS)

The Tinkers, or itinerants as they are now referred to, were regular periodic visitors to Loughglynn. They generally came in autumn time when horse drawn caravans used to converge from every direction. The caravans were no more than a flat cart covered with a tarpaulin where they kept their bedding, clothes and cooking utensils and tents. They occupied the waste land in 'long acre' outside our school. The grass verges of the avenue was a favourite venue on which to pitch their tents. The travellers eked out a living by collecting scrap metal, old clothes or anything else they could lay their hands on, and selling simple wares such as the saucepans which they had made. Some of them were horse dealers who took to the road in the summer and autumn months – the pie-bald horses trailed behind the caravans and carts and were herded along by wild looking tinker youths who also used to ride them bare-back cowboy fashion. Goats, donkeys and the dogs trailed behind them. The Convent Avenue was unfenced at the time and there were no houses there except Villa Maria, the convent chaplain's residence, so there was plenty of room and plenty of fodder for the horses, goats and donkeys. Firewood was readily available from the woodlands, and they were adept at snaring rabbits or hares for food. They were generally looked on with suspicion partly because of their undeserved reputation for thieving and partly because of their strange appearance. They all had large families. The tinker children were sharp as a needle, bright-eyed and always had an eye on the main chance. The majority couldn't read or write, although occasionally some of them (to our delight) would appear in the classroom, take a look at the set-up, and disappear like bats out of hell. On our way to school in the morning we used to stare with envy at these children as they sat on upturned pots and pans skinning rabbits, playing with their dogs, or making fishing rods from sallies in the woods. They glared back at us and spoke in a patois which was unintelligible, the spit, which nearly always used to miss us, conveyed their contempt of our boring existence. After all, they were doing all the things we longed to do and they didn't have to go to school; above all, they didn't have to be neat and tidy. As far as we were concerned, they had an idyllic existence.

The tinker women, old and young, wore shawls, the elderly favoured black ones, the younger women wore gaudy plaid ones, their skirts and dresses were always ankle length. Nearly all of them had glorious red or yellow blond hair reaching to their shoulders. They favoured pig-tails. On fair days they always visited the local town of Ballagh. They carried their babies inside their shawls and begged in a low whining voice, rising to a crescendo of obscenities if you refused them. They sold ballad sheets and some of the more enterprising sang haunting ballads in the Irish language. Apparently the songs were part of tinker lore and culture and stated that the travelling people were Ireland's true aristocrats who were forced to flee to the mountains when they were dispossessed. They were still waiting for their lost heritage. The travelling men who were lithe and swarthy, nearly always sported bandannas and carried a wooden tool-box on their backs. On fair days they galloped bare-backed through the town or drove along in flat carts, traps, or hand made hoop covered caravans similar to the covered wagons in America's wild west. They tethered their horses outside the pubs or bars and in the evening were joined by their women-folk. When they got tipsy, fighting would occasionally break out. I recall waiting for a bus at one of the pubs when a tinker woman rushed out followed by her husband. He grabbed her by her beautiful plaits and was about to thump her when a passer-by intervened, and pinned the itinerant to the wall while somebody ran for garda assistance. The tinker's wife promptly picked up her husband's ash-plant and smashed it several times across her benefactor's head, felling him to the ground. "You lave my man alone" she screamed, "or I'll break every tooth in your ugly puss". She and her husband returned to the pub arm in arm. The benefactor had a very sore head. The return of the tinker and his wife was a signal for a full time tinker battle. The factions took sides, but it was strictly tinker business. The fight went on with no holds barred, fists, knees, boots, heads, ash plants, the lot; the garda generally arrived as the battle tailed off. The travelling community were an integral part of the fair day in Ballagh.

When they had organised their living quarters and settled in, the tinkers would visit the local people. The women and children usually came first laden with shiny tin mugs or saucepans about pint size. The saucepans were handy because in our house we were always short of china because of breakages. I can still taste the tea or cocoa from these tinker mugs, it had a peculiar metallic taste. After a few days, the solder which kept them together weakened and they fell to bits. In return for these mugs my mother would barter basics such as tea, sugar, potatoes, lamp oil and sometimes a piece of bacon if it was round pig killing time. The tinker children would squat sullenly on the floor and stare suspiciously at us. The tinker men, who described themselves as tin-smiths, generally called later in the day. My mother collected all the leaking saucepans, kettles and pots to be mended (nothing was ever thrown away). The tinker man would open his tool chest and put the array of equipment on the floor. He had solder, tiny chisels, a very big scissors like instrument, and a sheet of shiny tin which was flexible. He would then examine the faulty kettles and pans, measure the holes and cut out two circles of tin which we called 'penny tinkers'. He would solder them inside and outside the hole, leave it to dry for a few minutes, and hey presto, the pot didn't leak any more. Many of the tinker men were horse dealers, and my father who was a cattle jobber at one time would talk endlessly about the fairs up and down the country. The horse fair in Ballinasloe was a favourite topic, and it was fascinating to hear the inside story of the wheeling and dealing that went on at these fairs. The tinkers always ended up trying to sell my father one of their pie-bald horses. "They're no good for the plough" my father said, but the tinker maintained that, like himself, they were the aristocrats of the equine population. He used to go into great detail of the breeding process in order to produce the super pie-bald horse variety. I only wish I had written it down.

The Gypsies or Romanies were a different race from the tinkers, and very rarely had anything to do with them. There was no intermarrying or assimilation between both tribes The gypsy horse-drawn caravans were of elaborate barrel vaulted design and were decorated with bright colours and traditional Romany motifs. They were a sheer delight to look at and I can still see in my mind's eye a swarthy gypsy man sitting on the shafts of the caravan on an autumn evening playing haunting tunes on a ukulele in the moonlight. The aromatic smoke of the woodfire which consisted of beech, oak, silver birch, pine and chestnut was intoxicating. The gypsies were superb whistlers. They used this skill to great advantage to summon their children, and their horses or to warn them of danger. The men were mostly horse traders and they used to wash and groom their horses at the sluice.

The gypsy women were swarthily beautiful. They dressed in gaudy clothes and wore huge gold looped earrings. They made and sold crêpe paper flowers, clothes pegs and willow baskets. They also told fortunes. Their initial gypsy formula was 'I'll tell your future if you cross my palm with silver'. The silver was a minimum of three-pence and you didn't get much for that, it had to be a tanner (six pence) for reasonable value. They generally targeted the young girls and promised them that when they crossed the water they would marry a tall dark handsome millionaire. The astute gypsies guessed that most of us would be taking that path. The crêpe flowers were garish but colourful, and appealed to us children. I remember throwing away a bunch of wild flowers which were in front of the Sacred Heart picture and replacing them with the gypsy crêpe paper ones. The gypsy women sometimes used their caravans for fortune telling. Generally it was the older women who went surreptitiously to the vans. They were scathing about it when the young ones had their fortunes told, calling it 'pishogues', but deep down they had a yearning to know what the future had in store. They were also very curious to know what the caravans were like inside. For weeks a catalogue of the vans' contents was talked about – silver, glass, and 'valuable' paintings of 'foreign' parts. The gypsies usually came from the north, so Donegal and Antrim were "the foreign parts". The husbands used to say 'How did they come by that lot?' and the general opinion was 'They'd built a nest in your ear'. Despite the scepticism about the fortune tellers, their powers of clairvoyance was believed to be uncanny. I remember how the women would recall how years ago an old gypsy had told them many things that had come true – for instance, their daughter would marry a dark (rich) man across the seas – a long journey, a piece of good fortune – a death within a year – all predictable in the midst of life. At that time, no matter who you married overseas was thought to be rich and powerful. The gypsies referred to us country folk as 'gorgios'. I always got the impression that they looked down on us, and that they as a result of their travelling and the gypsy lore and skills had the edge on us.

Nevertheless, the gypsies and tinkers were an integral part of life in my youth. True they were a nuisance - they occasionally made a mess. They were looked on with suspicion, but then at that time it was partly the ancient villagers' fear of strangers and foreigners coming among us. However, as all travellers, they brought a breath of fresh air, a new dimension and certainly a talking (and grumbling) point into our lives. When they visited our homes, besides mending the pots and pans they talked about far away places. They never visited a doctor and told us about the medicinal properties of herbs. They also told us about their adventures and the harassment which they invariably suffered. They generally slept in tents, and one tinker visitor told us that one night when a group of ramblers were returning home, on passing the tent they noticed a bare bottom protruding. One of the boys who was a pipe smoker placed the hot pipe which had a tin lid on the bare bottom. The ramblers looked on it as fun, but the tinker who was on the receiving end swore vengeance on them if he caught them. They lived mainly an outdoor life. They sat around their tents and caravans making wares to sell, skinning rabbits and hares, and preparing delicious stews with wild herbs which would put the food programmes on today's television to shame. They were a colourful addition to fair days in Ballagh, the plaid shawls and yellow hair of the tinker women contrasted sharply with the rather drab black attire worn by country women at the time. The squabbles, the begging, the ballad singing, but above all the independence of the travellers to engage in a way of life which on the face of it was extremely difficult, but which they obviously enjoyed because they valued the freedom it brought more than riches and wealth, earned them a grudging respect. When I return home now I feel nostalgic for the tinkers and gypsies of my youth – especially the elegant tinker woman who, after a few drinks, sang the haunting melody 'Lay my head beneath a rose' and who told the story of how she eloped from wealthy farming stock to follow the swarthy swashbuckling tinker man along the winding dusty roads of Ireland, the roads that for the travelling people had no end.

In today's Ireland, the travelling people of my youth have vanished. They have purpose-built motorised caravans, and are entitled to benefits from a modern welfare state. Some of them are accommodated in state built houses with all the mod cons. The colourful shawls have gone, and the huge hooped earrings. Today's tinker girls wear regulation blue jeans and probably never saw a shiny tin saucepan. Making baskets from willows and artificial flowers from crépe paper have no place in the money based economy of modern Ireland – sadly the itinerants in their compounds seem to be part of it.

THE MISSION

Every three years at autumn time we had a mission in Loughglynn Church just when the nights were lengthening and all the harvest was gathered in. We were reminded constantly about this important event by our parish priest and curate. Like every other event, religious or secular, the mission was a semi-social as well as a religious occasion. It brought new people into the village, the stall-holders and the Redemptorist priests. The stall holders arranged the stalls at the church gate; they were very colourful and were lit by Tilly lamps – holy pictures formed the background. They were mainly pictures of Our Lady centred around the Sacred Heart. The Redemptorist Fathers had a special devotion to Our Lady of Perpetual Succour, so the picture was prominently displayed. The multi-coloured rosary beads, the holy medals, the brown and green scapulars, the prayer books with the shiny covers and their little metal clasps reminded us of Knock shrine which we visited every August 15th, the feast of the Assumption of Our Lady and gave a holiday atmosphere to the occasion. The Mission started at approximately 7.30 p.m. as this was before Vatican 2, there was no evening mass, so the sermons started straight away. They were delivered by the Redemptorist Fathers, each preaching on alternate evenings. The initial sermon admonished us all to prepare ourselves for the next world. "Death comes like a thief in the night", he thundered, "and our main purpose in this world which he referred to as "this vale of tears", was only to build up treasure in Heaven, an interval until judgement day, when we would be hurled into the hell of the damned if we were found wanting. This happy state of eternal bliss hereafter (not now) could be achieved only by prayers, fasting and alms deed", he said. He was pleased to see all the big families gathered at the Mission, and was fond of saying 'every baby is born with a loaf of bread under its arm'. Damme said an old farmer, I've had fifteen childer and thirty grand childer an' not wan o' them had as much as a crumb under his arm when he arrived. With the price of cattle and pigs as they are today at rock bottom, I'm finding it very hard to make ends meet at all. At the last fair I wasn't even bid for the two yearling calves. It's taking me all me time to survive in this world never mind thinking about the next all the time, said another father of ten. Tis true what ye're all saying, but the bit that puzzled me was the alms deeds. Oh, that means that you share all you have with the poor. What poor is he talking about, aren't we all poor – does he realise how bad the times are, nothing coming in and prices rising every day. The important thing is to look after our souls for the day we meet 'the man above' who gives the best place in Heaven to the poor and the needy. Missioner number two didn't even mention prayers, fasting, or giving alms, he concentrated instead on the 6th and 9th commandments. You'd think he went up the mountain with Moses the way he went on about them. He always began with the 6th commandment. "The sixth commandment forbids all immodest thoughts and desires, and all wilful pleasure in them", he intoned. Company keeping was, according to him, a grave sin, especially if you wandered into secluded spots and indulged in kissing, and touching and caressing intimately. Desiring these things and finding wilful pleasure in these evil thoughts was 'a blue print' for the high road to Hell and eternal damnation, so you were damned if you did, and damned if you didn't. Parents were ordered to keep a strict eye on their sons and daughters and not encourage promiscuity. He also advised parents to discourage their children from emigrating to Britain, as he said "England is not Protestant any more, but Pagan". Where will our children go if we don't send them to England, only for the money we get every fortnight from our Mick we couldn't manage at all, said n old farmer. Missing the Mission was tantamount (in our family at least) to committing a mortal sin. One evening I was very late as I had to cycle from Ballagh in the dark without a bicycle light. They were all coming out of the church as I jumped off my bike dismayed. I was desperate to know what the missioner was preaching about that evening. I met an old lady, a great friend of mine who always boasted that she took everything they said 'with a pinch of salt'. What was he on about tonight, Bridget, I said, Mammy'll want to know, she couldn't go tonight. He was giving out about the fires o' hell an you'd take your oath, he was bred, born and raised there the way he went on about it, an' if we didn't change our sinful ways we'll all end up there.

The Mission wasn't all doom and gloom and hell fire, it had its lighter side as well. One evening a gang of men were coming home from the fair slightly tipsy. One of them in the parlance of the day was 'paralytic'. They decided to go to the Mission, but they picked a bad night because it was the renewal of baptismal vows evening and every person in the church had to hold a lighted candle during this ceremony in order to renounce the devil and all his works and pomps. One of the men from the fair (the paralytic one) slumped in the pew and fell fast asleep. His friends thought it was best to let sleeping farmers lie, and left him. Suddenly the church which was normally very dark (it was the pre-electric light age) became illuminated with candlelight and all the people stood to renew their vows. The noise wakened Johnny – it was a rude awakening, you could hear a pin drop in anticipation of the ceremony. When Johnny saw the illuminations through bleary eyes he got an awful fright, he jumped up shouting 'Begob boys, I've snuffed it and landed in Heaven. Look at all the lovely candles an' all the angels holding them. I'm dead so I am, it's great in Heaven. He started to sing at the top of his drunken voice, "Don't you wish you were bloody well dead?' The Missioner for once was gob-smacked, but he shouted him down and asked "Do you renounce the devil with all his works and pomps?' 'I do the bugger" said Johnnie. Johnnie's friends dragged him out amid muffled laughter, snuffed candles, dripping candle grease and an irate missioner yelling about the evils of drink and drunkards. It's a change from the ould sex bit anyway, everyone agreed. The incident of Johnny "rising from the dead" was talked and laughed about long after the Missioner's diatribe was forgotten.

A disturbing part and aftermath of the mission was the way courting couples were hounded by the clergy. The priests followed young couples around and scolded them for company keeping, and loitering with each other about the roads. Dance halls were in vogue at the time, the traditional 'house dances' were dying out and the new halls replaced them. One priest had a habit of visiting the dances and separating couples who appeared to be dancing too close with the crook of his umbrella. The clergy were also scathing about newspapers and books that told stories about love and romance. These were 'an occasion of sin', they said. Most of the time the people listened, accepting the priest's opinion about everything. However, when one mother was visited by the clergy and warned to put a stop to her daughter's company keeping, she countered by asking the priest himself a question. "Tell me Father, she said, how do you think you managed to get into this world? I take it you have a father and a mother?" He got quite indignant and said, "Of course I have – the best parents in the world, God bless them". "Quite", she said, "but if the priest ordered them to stop courting, where would that leave you Father". 'If he was stuck he wouldn't give blood', she said. he turned on his heel and took himself off. I put him in his place, she crowed triumphantly. The courting couple concerned married and had a wonderfully happy life together. It was the best of times, and it was the worst of times. Awkward situations were always saved by humour – the safety valve of our village and our nation. That particular Mission was always remembered as the night Johnny rose from the dead.

THE STATIONS

The stations, or having mass celebrated in one's home, was and is a tradition handed down from the penal days in Ireland when there was a price on every priest's head and mass had to be offered in secluded places behind hills and rocks; this is said to be the origin of the mass rock. The men formed a circle or bodyguard at the periphery of the mass venue in order to alert the priest in the event of a swoop by British military. In my youth this tradition continued in catholic churches. With the exception of 'the big Knob' as we used to refer to the upper echelons of our society, the men still knelt at the back of the church, and after mass they gathered outside the church gates and put the world to rights. I was amazed when I worked in London to see that my fellow Irish men emigrants clung to this tradition and on Sunday morning they could be seen kneeling reverently in the porch (and outside) Westminster Cathedral, taking part in the mass. It was a great link with home. To return to the stations, they were a major event in every village. It was considered an immense privilege. An old lady who was requested by the parish priest to 'take the stations' out of her turn because her neighbours who were returning to America could not avail of the honour. 'Glory be to God, Father, am I have to have that blessed privilege, blessed and praise be His holy name. Sure, I'll have to start getting the house ready. I have the rheumatics very bad but sure, all the neighbours will help me.' We didn't need to be told, that was a signal to start the big 'clean up'. No task force took the work so seriously. Like every other event of my youth, there was a social aspect to the stations preparation. Furniture that hadn't been moved since the Yanks came visiting two years previously was pulled out. I remember moving an enormous grain bin with the help of my friends. The grain bin was used to store flour, oatmeal, bran and other foodstuffs for people and animals. A nest of mice rushed out, to be immediately pounced on by Tom the big farmyard cat. One of the mice ended up in a crock of cream in the loft. When Tom pounced, both the crock, the mouse and the cat ended in a sea of cream on the flagged kitchen floor. 'God blast ye to hell' said old Ellen, 'that was the crame that was goin' to be churned that was goin' to make the butter for the priest's breakfast. Hell won't be full until that divil of a cat's in it', she said. All the piety and prayers about the blessed privilege of the mass was forgotten in her tirade against the tom cat. 'You're an old hypocrite Ellen' I said, 'if the Canon heard you he wouldn't be so keen on letting you have holy mass in the house'. Divil a notice he'd take as long as me and the villagers pay him his dues, mark my words, said Ellen. When all the pictures and calendars that dated back to the jolly nineties were removed and dusted, Ellen was sitting in the middle of the floor hugging a life sized photograph. Tears were pouring down her wrinkled face as she gazed at the sad emaciated face of a young girl. This is my poor Annie, she wailed, the best looking girl in the parish when our Paddy paid her passage to Brooklyn. He wrote and said it was God's own country and that she was wasting her time in this God forsaken place. So she went off to Amerikay and left me. By all accounts she got a great job as a servant in a big house in Long Island. She was only there six months when she took bad with the lung sickness. Within the year she was dead, that was the sort of riches she got – a pauper's grave in a Bronx churchyard where they tell me that even the old weeds don't grow because of the muck. Emigration is an awful curse, she said, ye're better off to stay at home even if you have to ate praties and salt than goin' to foreign parts where no wan knows you. My Annie died of a broken heart, an' she's bruk mine as well. She continued to reminisce. Every wan o' me chider, all ten o' them are scattered all over the world, one in America, three in Australia, one in Quebec, and the rest in Liverpool, England. No wan left to comfort me in me ould age, we have to keep goin' while we're in it, she said as she jumped up, wiped a tear from her eye with her flour bag apron, and began to vigorously mix the whitewash in the big white pail. We all started on different walls, splashing and splodging. We covered the dresser and the wag-at-the-wall clock with sheets to protect them from the splashes; there was whitewash everywhere in the middle of all this. Dan arrived with his piano accordion. The work was done to a musical accompaniment – the sound of music brought in more of the neighbours who sang, recited, told stories and made tea. Limewash has a pristine whiteness about it, an outdoor refreshing early morning tang like the air on a headland. The big old kitchen was transformed as we polished and replaced the ancient pictures, nearly all of which were evocative of the past for old Ellen. The sheets were taken from the dresser and the delft glinted and danced in the soaring firelight. The soft glow of the hanging lamp lent a peacefulness to the scene as Tom brought in the sacred box which contained the priest's vestments, and holy vessels for the morning's Holy Sacrifice. We laid the table in the parlour for the morning's breakfast. The china was borrowed from a relative, a neighbour brought in the golden 'butter balls' when she heard about the cream disaster, but the triumph of the priest's breakfast table was the sugar lumps and the sugar tongs, lent by a posh neighbour who returned from Boston and married a local farmer. Aren't they just dandy, said Ellen, just imagine me, ould Ellen O'Leary with silver sugar tongs, that'll show the canon and the curate that we come from good stock, even if the silver is borrowed. He's not to know, but every wan knows that we're descended from the noble kings of Connaught. We bade goodnight to Ellen not before we covered "the wag of the wall" clock to make sure she was up early in the morning to receive the Canon. We wended our way homeward underneath a star-studded sky. As I lifted the latch in our house the moon was rising. I hope Ellen wakes up, I prayed.

The next morning we were all assembled outside Ellen's house for the station mass. Tradition decreed that the canon and his curate entered the station house first. The station mass was scheduled for 8.30 a.m. The people were waiting on the boreen for the canon and curate to arrive. They were a little bit late, but soon the old baby Austin could be heard chug-chugging up the boreen. "They're here", we all whispered. The canon helped out of the car by the curate walked up the pathway to the door of Ellen's cottage. The canon banged on the door with his folded umbrella several times but there was no immediate response. What's wrong with Ellen?, I said anxiously. The canon was getting impatient, he banged harder on the door. Suddenly it opened and Ellen appeared in a long, dishevelled night-gown. She was very perturbed and anxious, as she explained "I wasn't expecting you so early, canon, will you do me a favour your reverence. Lift up me petticoat an' look at the clock'. We all gasped, as we remembered that we put ould Ellen's red petticoat over the wag at the wall clock so that it would keep perfect time for the morning. The canon who was a courteous and tactful man said "Good morning Ellen'. Good morning canon, said Ellen in great agitation. Lift up me petticoat canon and look at the clock. You understand canon, it didn't chime when it should have done. I understand, Ellen, he said as he beckoned us all to come in to Ellen's station mass.

CHAPTER TWELVE

LOUGHGLYNN SCHOOL IN THE THIRTIES AND FORTIES

As we have seen Loughglynn school was built in 1850 on the periphery of Viscount Dillon's estate, at the prompting of Charles Strickland who acted as agent for Lord Dillon in his absence. The school consisted of four classrooms, two large classrooms (the big rooms) and two smaller ones. There was a boys' school and a girls' school and each school had its own principal teacher and two assistant teachers. It was enclosed by iron railings, and both schools were partitioned by railings. The playground was 'grassed over', two ancient yew trees stood in each playground and laburnum, copper beech and pine trees provided a wind break in winter and shady spots in summer. The yew tree was the venue for all us 'scholars'. It was our 'dining room' where we ate our soda bread sandwiches, with various fillings like rhubarb, apple or marrow jam, it was there we organised our games and it was there that we learned our poetry for Friday afternoon poetry sessions. I remember one girl saying, When I die and go to purgatory, (everyone has to go to purgatory before they get to Heaven), I'll pray to you all, "have pity on me, have pity on me, at least you lot at the yew tree".

I vividly recall my first day at school – my sisters brought me. The infants, junior and senior, plus first and second class were

Loughglynn Girls School circa 1934–1935. Can you find yourself?

accommodated in the small room, which was referred to as "the classroom". We were given two reading books, an Irish primer and an English primer. I was fascinated by the brown wainscot, and the mouse that kept darting in an out of a hole just next to my desk. He ws totally unafraid and nibbled away at my new friends' sandwiches. If our cat Topsy was here, you wouldn't be doing that for long m'lud, I thought. On the muddy dark green painted wall over the wainscot were nursery rhyme pictures. Look at that 'ould' cow jumpin' over the moon, said my friend, doesn't she look a right eejit. We both laughed delightedly. A sharp tap on the desk stopped our laughter. Pay attention now, said our teacher as she introduced us to the alphabet, and our academic lives had begun. Each year we were 'put up' to the next class, or 'kept down' if we failed to reach the heights of academia. Our first confession, and our first Holy Communion were the highlights of the classroom. We had to be familiar with and be able to recite the penny Catechism "who made the world?" "Who made you?" "How many Gods are there?" We also had to learn the ten Commandments, and the seven deadly sins by rote. Mortal sin killed the soul by depriving it of sanctifying grace and merited Hell for all eternity. This grievous sin must be told in Confession. You only ended up in purgatory if you committed a 'venial sin'. We practised the Confession format with the teacher. 'Bless me Father, for I have sinned'. The teacher warned us to tell all our 'mortal' sins first, but don't tell them to me, because the Priest acts for God and all our sins are secret. He can't even tell anyone else about them. The great day came and I went to confess my sins to the Canon who was slightly deaf. I was taking no chances, no way did I want to end up in Hell for ever and ever, so I started off 'Bless me Father for I have sinned. This is my first confession'. Tell me your sins, child. I reeled off very fast, 'pride, covetousness, lust, anger, gluttony, envy and sloth'. Very good, you have made up your mind never to commit these sins again. Now say an act of contrition to show you're sorry. 'O my God'. God bless you and pray for me. I came out beaming, it was easy. A few weeks later I was very naughty at home and my big sister said to me, that's a sin, you'll have to tell it in Confession. I don't so, I said. Our teacher

Loughglynn Girls School circa 1937–1938
Mrs Kenny (teacher in doorway). Junior and senior infants, first and second classes.
Left to right, top row: Kathleen Delaney, Mary Scolly, Gretta Casey, Kathleen Fitzpatrick, Mary McDermott, Noreen Crawley, Pauline Gilligan, Mary Toe Fitzpatrick, Teresa Maloney, Una, Maura McDermott.
Middle row: Mena Towey, Angela McGeever, Mary K Barrett, Brenda Kelly, Maura O'Connor, Laura McDermott, Annie M Regan, Teresa Scally, Teresa McGreal.
Seated: Peggy Mulrennan, Una Crawley, Annie Heneghan, Annie Beirne, Gretta Finan, Mary Connolly, Doris Flanagan, Maeve Kelly, - - -P Crawley.
Bridie Burke next to P Gilligan (top row) Next to Annie May Regan – Vera McDermott.

'learned us' our sins, and I reeled off the seven deadly ones. You'll go to Hell for sure now you've told lies in Confession. She wagged her finger at me menacingly. I bawled my head off. I don't want to go to hell. "What's all the bawling" said mammy, as she came in the back door. She's only disgraced us in Confession, said big sister, she's been telling the seven deadly sins to the Canon. I wouldn't worry, said my dad, she's probably tried out a few already. "You'll go to Hell, you'll go to Hell for all eternity" chanted my big sisters, with great glee. Mammy comforted me and took me back to the Canon who was very amused when he heard the tale. "Don't tell me teacher" I said, an' I'll never tell lies again in Confession. He looked at me solemnly and said, don't worry, we can never tell anyone, even your teacher what we are told in Confession. I can still hear him chuckling to himself as he sat on a chair by the marble altar rails in the Church at Loughglynn.

It was a great occasion when we moved into 'the big room'. Our teacher expected very high standards of us, she was a stickler for punctuality, (I don't recall her ever being late) so she expected the same from us, but we had a problem at home as we had only a wall clock that was bought at an auction. It was very temperamental and had to be placed at a certain angle on the wall in order to keep reasonable time. It was nearly always 'fast' or 'slow'. If it was 'fast' we'd race all the way to school, praying that we wouldn't be late; if it was 'slow' we'd dawdle thinking we had plenty of time. The road to school was via 'the ryde', a bridle track which was formerly used by the gentry for horse and carriage riding. It went through Sabbath wood which we referred to as 'the nun's wood'. In spring time it was carpeted with bluebells, primroses, and violets. The swathes of bluebells looked like miniature azure streams as they shimmered in the morning light. In autumn we kicked the carpets of fallen leaves as they fluttered from the trees and felt the first nip of winter in the air. The wood was home to rabbits, badgers, weasels and wild life of every description. We loved to hear the crk, crk of the corncrake on a summer's evening and to our great delight we found a corncrake's nest in the coarse grass by a stream. From a distance we observed the young birds being hatched, and were sad when they flew away. The corncrake is no longer heard in the meadows and woods at Loughglynn. On our way to school (if the clock was fast) we'd gather armfuls of dew-laden wild flowers and take them to our teacher. We filled jam jars with the scented blooms, and arranged them between the big scarlet geranium plants on the wide Victorian window sills, the bird song and the heady scent of the flowers brought the wild-wood into the classrooms. This idyllic interlude existed only if we were on time – if we were late the flowers wilted forlornly on the desk inside the door, reflecting our own mood as we made our feeble excuses. 'Please ma'am, our clock was slow and we thought we were early'. That's right, blame the clock, hold your hand out - the school day had begun.

Occasionally we had visitors at school. Sometimes past pupils who had emigrated to England or America came in to visit their Alma Mater. We loved these interruptions as we had a short break from lessons. The Inspector, or 'the Cigire' as our teacher refered to him, came at regular intervals, always unannounced. I remember vividly one afternoon I was summoned to the teacher's desk because I got all my long division sums wrong in the weekly test. She was angry as she spent a lot of time explaining the maths concept which I failed to grasp. The blackboard which she used to teach us was placed on the big window at the end of the room. This window looked out on a copper beech tree, where a blackbird built her nest year after year. My mind wandered as I watched the two birds working diligently, carrying twigs, hair and bits and pieces to build their home. I hated maths. "You were 'wool-gathering' instead of listening", she said, "even your father's donkey would have grasped it by now". I must be awful thick, I thought, if I'm worse than our ould Ted. My father used to say, I'd get rid of the lazy ould divil, only for the children like to ride him, he's good for nothing. I was saved by a knock on the door and the dreaded 'Cigire' walked in. I crept back to my desk – forgotten. We kids used to call him 'the black-and-tan' Inspector, he must have been forgotten when the British departed. He was nearly seven feet tall, and as thin as a lathe – a real string o' misery. He wore a black pin-striped suit, and carried a regulation rolled up black umbrella.

He was as bald as a coot, and when he spoke his pronounced Adam's apple bobbed up and down, as if it was trying to escape. He never spoke Gaelic like the jolly rollicking Inspector from Munster, who greeted us with "Is binne an gaelige ná port na fuisega" (Irish is sweeter than the song of the lark). The 'black an' tan Inspector didn't know any Irish, he was 'a geography man', as soon as he glanced at the roll book (register) and spoke briefly to our teacher, he picked up 'the pointer' and headed for the map of Europe. Our teacher always told us to put our hands up and look alert, and attempt the answer, even if we weren't sure of it. The pointer hovered around Italy, and eventually landed on the island of Sicily. Where does Sicily lie, he asked. He pointed to a girl by the name of Lizzie, whose mother's name was Cecilia, her 'pet name' was Cissie, or Cissly. Lizzie (not her real name) looked puzzled. Well, where does Sicily lie, he repeated somewhat menacingly. "Inside Paddy in the Pristy", she whispered. Speak up girl, he said. It was his turn to look puzzled. "Inside Paddy in the pristy", she shouted. Inside Paddy in the where? He turned to our teacher who was (uncharacteristically) covered in confusion. They had a brief whispered conversation, after which he made a hasty exit. Good riddance, we thought, our favourite Inspector would have known what a "pristy" was. When we told the story at home, they all roared with laughter. That'll teach the ould planter to go back to where he belongs.

The playground was grassed over. It was very pleasant in summer but it was very damp in winter. As I said earlier, we used to sit under the yew tree and eat our sandwiches - Cafferky's hens picked up the crumbs. It was a social occasion where we organised our playground games, but especially on a Friday, we used to revise our poetry for the afternoon session. The senior classes had to stand at the back of the class, and individually recite 'a set poem' which was assigned for homework. It was great for elocution but extremely nerve wracking. I vividly remember sitting in a group, frantically learning one of Douglas Hyde's poems. It went like this.

> Four sharp scythes sweeping in concert keeping the rich robed

meadow – broad bosom o'er.
Four strong men mowing with bright health glowing.
A long green sward, spread each man before.
With sinews springing – my keen blade swinging,
I strode – the fourth man in that blithe band.
As stalk of corn, that summer morn, the scythe felt light – in my stalwart hand.

Most of us found it hard to remember. We all wished we had put a bit more effort in the previous evening. Mary Jane – a friend of mine, said 'if only I didn't go to Jack's last night, card playin', I'd have learned it. Anyways I won the tanner and I'm goin' to buy that lucky package – a 'silver' bracelet that's been in King's window for ages". Lucky you, I said, I had my eye on that as well, but no luck. We were getting desperate, and one of the 'bright sparks', Josie Donovan, suggested we should try various strategies to divert the teacher. If she was in a good mood she'd spent a lot of time giving us background information about the poet. Hyde signed himself "An Craobhinn". One of the pupils generally opened the poetry book and gave it to Ma'am at the start of the lesson. Let's open it at the end of the poem where it says 'Craobhinn' said Josie – I'll ask her what it means and with any luck she'll blather on for ages about the similes and metaphors and theme. Just listen to this rubbish, said Josie, 'broad bosom o'er', if you ask me, it's downright rude – the Canon wouldn't like it. Why did he call himself "Crubeen' said Kate, another girl – that manes pig's feet. We have them every Saturday for our dinner. Never mind that, said Josie, if we keep her 'blatherin' she won't have time to hear us recite, an' we'll get off. Miss 'know all', one of the girls who never put her foot wrong and always did her homework, disagreed with Josies' strategy. She thought it was underhand and sly. She pointed out that 'An Craoibhinn' was the nom de plume used by Dr Douglas Hyde who was a native of Ratra and founded the Gaelic League. Our plan looked as if it was going to be scuppered, but we reckoned without Josie's blackmail tactics. She put her hands on her hips - "Miss Know All, if you as much as open your mouth, I'll tell your mother you walk up the sandy road every Friday night with Martin Farrell, and when you think there's no wan lookin' ye link him. An' if his mother finds out, God help ye, entirely, everyone knows she does the 'nine Fridays' so that God will give him a vocation for the priests. Miss Know All defeated - flounced off in high dudgeon, muttering about dunces and dumb-bells. Josie was cock-a-hoop. Madam won't say a word with that hangin' over her head, she said with great glee. The lesson went according to plan, our teacher with her blather brought Douglas Hyde, the Ratra people and the Frenchpark countryside to life on that sunny afternoon "in youths noontide" in the old school at Loughglynn. Another poem that we learned and that comes to mind, was Wordsworth's 'Daffodils'. "When all at once, I saw a crowd, a host of golden daffodils". Years later, as I was walking along a crowded street in London, I passed a Cockney flower seller standing in front of a barrow of daffodils chanting "Bootiful daffy's, a tanner a bunch". I was immediately back in the playground at Loughglynn, under the yew tree with my friends. Like the poet, I gazed and gazed, but little thought what wealth (and longings) the show to me had brought. Typical of Londoners, a queue began to form behind me. 'Move along there lidy, move along', said a young Cockney bobby, 'or ye'll find yerself in the arms of the law'. I was back again in the bleak London street, 'with hundreds of faces, not one that I know, but the cold of the wind on my face as I go'.

Usually the games we played were seasonal. In summer we sat on the concrete slab underneath the windows and played "jackstones". This game required a fair amount of skill and manual manipulation. It consisted of five small smooth stones, the quality and smoothness of the stones were important. Some of the more affluent scholars who went to the seaside for holidays usually brought back sets of beautiful rounded speckled stones from the Strandhill or Bundoran beaches. These stones were very sought after, and were often bartered for worthless objects like the 'silver' bracelet, or even an orange or a piece of chocolate. The more popular game was "Wall Flowers". We all danced round in a circle and chanted.

Wall flowers, wall flowers, growing up so high.

> All those young ladies are all sure to die.
> Except Vera McDermott, she's the best of all.
> She can skip and she can turn the candlestick.
> So turn your back to the wall again,
> and tell your sweetheart's name.

It was my turn to be asked who my sweetheart was. I didn't get a chance to choose, as one of the "big girls" chose for me. She had a grudge against a boy called Paddy Slattery. She decided with her friends that they were going to pull him down a peg. He struts about 'like a cock on a dunghill' and ignores us. He'll only talk to 'the Convent girls', the rest of us are beneath him – we'll show him, they said. The chanting continued, loud and clear.

> Paddy Slattery said he'd have her,
> All the boys are fighting for her,
> Let them say what they like,
> But Paddy Slattery has his wife.

When he heard his name chanted in connection with me, who was not only in the 5th class, but small with long straggly pigtails, he stood and glared from the boys' playground. Just then our teacher appeared at the door and clapped her hands. Playtime was over. I was standing near the railings. Suddenly I felt a tug on my plaits. I tried to free myself but Paddy Slattery had tied them to the railings. That'll larn ye, niver, niver to call me your sweetheart. Just look at ye, two hands higher than a duck, with your thin legs and your straggly plaits. Our teacher was clapping her hands frenziedly – Come into your line at once, she said. I can't, I sobbed, me plaits are tied to the railings. I dragged myself free at last only to be warned not to be 'intimate' with the boys. I didn't play 'wall flowers' again for a long time. The 'big girls' had their revenge, that's put that upstart Slattery in his place, they giggled.

In winter time, especially when we had frost and snow, we were allowed to eat our lunch in the classroom. Some senior girls were in charge of boiling the kettle on the turf fire, and pouring the water into our enamel cocoa mugs. We each had our own mug and our own cocoa. Sometimes if the cocoa ran out at home, we brought tea mixed with sugar. It always tasted of turf smoke mixed with ashes, but it was better than being out in the bleak playground under the dripping trees. After lunch a 'concert' was organised. Everyone was expected to contribute, but usually the extroverts took over. Occasionally we had the temerity to do a 'skit' on the teachers but we had to be very careful as RESPECT and DEFERENCE were the bywords for teachers, and indeed anyone in authority at the time. The slightest criticism even as a joke was frowned on.

Heating the school was the responsibility of the parents. Each year in September the 'heating list' would appear and our teacher would remind us that it was time to bring the statutory crate of turf, or alternatively to bring a half-a-crown (2/6) (twenty six pence in today's currency) in lieu of the turf, to defray heating expenses. This arrangement sounds very feasible, but in reality was not very practical. In today's affluent society 2/6d is a derisory sum, a 'crate' of turf also appears to be reasonable. However, in the thirties both jobs and money were in short supply, families were large and many fathers, in order to make ends meet, took the boat and headed for the harvesting in Yorkshire and Lincolnshire. They could not therefore bring the regulation turf and brought the 2/6d instead. This was hard to find as well. Another problem was a wet year, which made it extremely difficult to rear the turf, which ended up damp and soggy. Apart from these problems, we always seemed to have a good fire, and I cannot recall ever being very cold. In Spring the rooks used to build their nests in the school chimney, the rookery (which is still there) was in the ancient beech trees behind the Demesne wall. Our teacher used to clean the chimney with the help of the 'big' girls. She got a long brush handle and covered it with newspapers soaked in paraffin oil. She would then light it, and poke it up the chimney, a roaring fire ensued, burning twigs and leaves and soot cascaded on the stone hearth. Outside, sparks flew from the school chimney and made it look like a gigantic firework display. The thunderous noise of the burning soot and debris, coupled with the frenzied cawing of the rooks as they

Loughglynn Boys School circa 1944–1945. Can you find yourself?
Top row: P Regan - - - - J Regan - - S Mulrennan
Middle row: D McDermott, Thomas O'Connor, P Kilduff, - Regan –
Seated: - - - - P Cassidy, Beirne – TP Gilligan, Conrad Duffy, R Flanagan.

flapped about looking piteously at the relics of their cosy nests, made an exciting interlude in our school lives. The best part was that we missed the dreaded maths session. Each morning the fire had to be cleaned and laid, and girls from the village used to do this chore faithfully. They called in to the teacher's house in the morning and Peter the handy-man used to half fill a galvanized type bucket with red hot coals. Two girls would carry the bucket to school, and with the help of newspaper, paraffin and turf, they soon got a roaring fire going. This was grand for the rest of us, as the school was warm when we arrived for lessons. The 'fire girls' never complained, and we never had to face a cold classroom. It was a potentially dangerous task and surprisingly no one ever got burned, or had any accident from the fire. The 'lunch girl' used to boil the kettle, make the toast and 'wet' the tea for teacher's lunch. This was 'a prestigious chore' and the chosen hand-maid was usually reliable, sensible, and academically bright. I remember when a new girl called Mary Ellen was given the task. Initially she was nervous, the tea was kept in a tea caddy (it was pre tea-bag time), she scalded the tea pot and put two great fistfuls of tea into the elegant china pot. At home this was the usual procedure. Our teacher was horrified, the tea poured like treacle. 'Mary Ellen, do use the strainer provided. I like very weak tea'. Please Ma'am, mammy always gives it five minutes on the hob 'to draw'. Well I don't like 'stewed' tea, Mary Ellen. Please remember that in future. 'It was like water' Mary Ellen said afterwards, 'you couldn't drink it to save your life'.

At the end of the school year we were 'put up' to a new class. This promotion meant that we had to buy a new set of school books. The English readers were always exciting, as we didn't have access to a library, and new books were a rarity. One of the books was entitled "A Lad of the O'Friels". It told the story of a Donegal schoolboy who was similar to ourselves, and one we could identify with. "The Wind in the Willows" was a great favourite, as living partly in a wild wood ourselves, the animal characters were great fun. The Gaelic favourite was O'Conaires "Màsal beag dubh' and the poetry book was entitled "Blátha na bhfilt". A folklore collection was introduced by the government in the late thirties and early forties. This research gave us a real insight into local history, customs and beliefs.

In 1939 when Britain declared war on Germany, we saw our first aeroplane. We all stood with our teachers watching it fly very low over the school – it made a tremendous noise. I hope we remain neutral, said our teacher. If we do, said a young supply teacher, it's the first time we've been neutral since the Battle of Contarf. After Coventry was devastated by the Luftwaffe in 1940, two evacuees, a brother and sister from there, came to stay with a Loughglynn family. Both of them came to our school. We all loved Kathleen, and were intrigued with her English Midlands accent. She soon became more Irish than ourselves. Our teacher referred to her as "little miss Coventry" and made her very welcome, and never punished her – not that she ever did much wrong. When she first arrived, she used to dive under the desk when the Convent bells sounded for community prayers. 'Quick, get down, it's the siren – an air raid warning'.

Loughglynn Girls School circa 1944–1945. Can you find yourself?
Top row: M Flanagan, E Luby, N Callaghan, M Connolly, G Duffy, MS Connolly, B Towey, MS Earley.
Middle row: - - - - M Regan, P Flanagan, K Delaney, A Greevy, D Flanagan, - -
3rd row: E Luby, - - M Giblin, Imelda Duffy, - - C Earley, K Hanley, - A Beirne.

In the first few weeks she carried her gas mask and described the horrors of the devastation of Coventry, and how she and her family had to run for their lives through a blazing inferno, where the pavements were not enough to cook a meal. It was a miracle that they were alive. Kathleen was a great asset to our school. She had a beautiful singing voice, and always sang 'Play to me gypsy, the moon's high above, play me the serenade, the one I love'.

THE RELIGIOUS EXAM

The Religious examination always took place after Christmas. It was an important event in the school calendar, and we spent a great deal of time preparing for it. We were examined class by class, and a certificate with a Celtic design was awarded to outstanding (or lucky) pupils. We had a fair idea of the format, and generally rehearsed the answers we thought were most likely. I remember one examination vividly. The Priest examiner usually started off with "Who made you? "How many Gods are there?" One exam day one member of the class was absent. He asked Jane "How many Gods are there?" She answered in a sing-song voice, "In God there are three Divine persons, really distinct and equal in all things, the Father, the Son and the Holy Ghost". I didn't ask you that, he said crossly. I know you didn't Father, Brigid should have answered that questions but she's off sick today. It wasn't his day – he asked another girl "What is the 9th Commandment?" She answered promptly, "9th, thou shalt not cover thy neighbour's wife". You mean 'covet' not cover. Well, it all comes to the same thing Father, don't it, she riposted. The hymn singing was hilarious, individual children were asked to sing solo, generally a Christmas carol or a hymn to Our Lady. The examiners' favourite hymn was about the Shepherds visiting the Infant Jesus. He asked this girl called Anne to sing the hymn. 'While shepherds watched', she began in a pitched nasal voice - 'While shepherds washed their socks at night'. He didn't fare any better with the hymns to Our Lady. 'O Mother, I could creep the earth'. He was an irascible little man with a nervous twitch, and a squint which gave the impression that he was looking at you when he was really looking at someone else. Like the 'black and tan' Inspector, he was short on charisma and humour. The religious examination day could have been fun but was spoiled by the disappointment of children who tried very hard but got no reward in the shape of a certificate with a Celtic design.

ELECTION DAY AT SCHOOL

We always looked forward to election day, even though we had to attend school, whereas the boys had a holiday as their school was used as the polling station. It was a semi-holiday for us. Early in the morning, the election caravan would arrive - the ballot boxes, the presiding officers, the poll clerks, the Garda, the candidates and their supporters, plus all the posters and flags paraphernalia. There were usually three parties – Fianna Fail, de Valera's party was the main one, the opposition was Fine Gael, and a third party set up on behalf of the farmers was called

'Clann na Talman'. The arguments between the opposition parties used to occasionally become very heated. Our teacher acted as hostess to the canvassers, most of the 'big girls' were busy making tea and sandwiches for them. The rest of us were attempting to work, but we had an eye glued on the excitement at the school gates. The Irish tricolour and posters of the Easter rising martyrs were flown from the trees along the Demesne wall, on behalf of the Fianna Fail party. The other parties were more muted, but the farmers or "Clann na Talman' had a poster of a charging bull and a logo that said "Vote for the farmers' friends "Clann na Talman'. It was immediately dubbed 'The Bull Party' by the older generation who found it difficult to get their tongues around the Gaelic 'Clann na Talman". Transport was provided for the elderly or for people who thought they were entitled to V.I.P. treatment. At one election an old man and his missus arrived on horseback, the horse was a bony old hack. The missus was very hefty, and an election candidate for the Farmers' party arrived at that minute and had to help her dismount. He did so with considerable exertion, the perspiration was pouring down his face as she touched the ground and re-arranged her hat and scarf. "I trust ye'll give me your vote, ma'am" he gasped. She gave him a withering look and said "Give you me vote, I'd see ye in Hell first, where wor ye when the fightin' was on? Under the bed, that's where – you ould humbug. Look at ye with your brilliantine an' ye'r polished shoes, an' your mothor car – far from them ye were raired". Hush missus, said her meek little husband. Hush yerself, she said. The Fianna Fail supporters cheered. 'That's right, you tell him, missus, we'll see ye right'. Off she went to cast her vote, singing "Wrap the green flag round me boys, to be my winding sheet". The little candidate who had recovered a little from his ordeal muttered, 'it'd have to be a bloody big windin' sheet to cover your carcass, you ugly ould bat'. It's a good job she didn't hear you say that said ould Jimmy. Even the 'auxies' used to run a mile when she put her head out.

The ass and trap was a favourite mode of conveyance. One old farmer decided to whitewash his vehicle and adorn it with pictures of animals cut out of farming magazines. The focal point was of course a bull, to complete the picture of elegance. He drove up and down the road cracking his whip, like the old landlords – pausing to give a lift to any aspiring voter for his party, which was "Clann na Talman". The bull logo was in a prominent position. He offered two very elegantly dressed canvassers for the Farmer's party, a lift.' They took one look at the equipage and exclaimed "Goodness me, you don't surely expect us to ride in that outfit. Get off with ye'. Swift as lightning he tore town the bull poster and replaced it with the republican tricolour. He trotted down to the school gate shouting, 'I've always been a Dev man. I wasn't afeared o'fighting.' You're an ould turn-coat' said a Fianna Fail canvasser, 'but keep that flag flyin'.' Election day was fun, and was one of the memorable highlights of school life in the thirties.

CHAPTER THIRTEEN
THE ROAD TO BALLAGH TOWN

In 1933 the Irish Sisters of Charity who had come to the town in 1877 opened a secondary school for the education of post-primary girls in Ballaghadereen and its environs. At that time second level education was not 'free'. The fees were £10 per annum. In today's context this is a derisory sum but in the thirties and forties to many it represented a fortune, especially as families were large and times weren't good. A County scholarship was available for a free place so one hot day in June I set off for St Joseph's school and had a 'stab' at the exam. It was written and oral and I vividly remember reciting a poem called *The death of Robert Emmett*.

> See there within the heart of Dublin City
> A silent throng of people waiting – Why?
> Because a noble soul, oh, tale of pity
> Comes forth today for freedom's cause to die
> He saw his country scourged and bruised and beaten
> and trampled down – a butt for brutal scorn
> Because he tried her sorrow draught to sweeten
> In manhood's budding strength, he died that morn

In September the Loughglynn contingent headed for Ballagh to start their academic education at one or other of three schools.

Some of my friends and myself went to St Joseph's. The journey was an exercise in resourcefulness and sociability. The roads were practically empty except for farmers in donkey carts taking milk to the creamery, and carting home the hay and turf to the haggards. World War II was raging, and bicycles and bicycle tyres were almost impossible to get hold of, so we always carried a puncture kit in a little yellow tin box. It consisted of a tube of "solution" and rubber patches of various shapes and sizes. A bicycle pump was also vital. Mending a puncture was a work of art, the bike had to be upended, the tyre had to be levered off with a kitchen fork or any other handy implement, the inner tube had to be removed, pumped up and placed in a bowl of water, a bubble indicated where the puncture was, the patch had to be stuck on very fast and the tube and tyre replaced and re-inflated. naturally we needed help with this operation and the help was given freely by the people in the villages through which we passed. They didn't think anything about leaving a field of corn or hay and giving us a hand with the bikes. We exchanged gossip and banter, time was there to be enjoyed. A favourite expression was "the 'man' who made time made plenty of it" and as the fragrant smell of the new mown hay wafted towards us the long summer days seemed to last for ever.

Shannon's Cross was the favourite venue for the budding scholars. Across the years I can still see "Fair girls, riding their bikes, and making the roads resound with the laugh and glee". The road mender at the time was a friendly sociable man who usually had his brazier burning at a very bleak part of the road. It was a welcome sight especially on frosty winter mornings when we all stopped and warmed our freezing hands in front of the glowing coals. In autumn his wife used to give us beautiful red juicy apples from the orchard in front of their house. "It was the best of times, it was the worst of times". The ramshackle bikes were museum pieces (at least mine was) but somehow we managed with a lot of help from our friends to reach school at 9.30 a.m. where we were met by our head teacher, the late Sr. Mary Martin MacLaughlin.

Sr. Martin was a Dublin woman, but she loved the west and its people and took them to her heart. She was a great scholar and

Senior Leaving Cert class 1947.
Left to right, back row: Noreen McCormack, Maureen Regan, Bernadette Maxwell, Nuala Quirke, Tessie Maxwell, Bernadette Durcan, Rita McGeever, front row: Mary Morrisroe, Vera McDermott, Una Morrisroe, Brenda Quirke.

teacher, a very great lady and an exemplary Sister of Charity. The Order was founded by Mother Mary Aikenhead who specified that the nuns went out among the people and gave help when it was needed. The motto of the Order, which was also the motto of our school "Caritas Christi urget nos", was practised to the letter by Sister Martin. She referred to us as "her daughters". Sometimes she found it difficult to understand our West of Ireland phraseology. I remember one morning four of us were late. Out excuse was "Vee an gee im aye". one of the teachers who overheard us remarked dryly, 'there must be a whirlwind this morning sister. It was against them from Loughglynn, Frenchpark, Carracastle *and* Monasteraden. The public examinations used to be held in St Mary's Hall. We examinees met at St Joseph's and Sr. Martin would escort us to the venue. On the way we recited the Rosary aloud much to the amusement of the Ballagh residents, especially some of the youths who used to meet us at 'dances', (the leaving Cert. girls were 17+ years). We

Leaving Cert class (1947) Re-union 1997. Left to right: Attracta Drury, May Rushe, Vera McDermott, Nora McCormack, Bernadette Maxwell, Maureen Regan.. Photograph courtesy of the Western People

knew exactly what the comment would be at the next 'hop': 'She'll never make a nun out of any of ye, it's the order of Dick, two heads on a tick for the lot of ye'.

Sr. Martin was always concerned about our physical as well as our spiritual welfare. In winter when the weather was very inclement we used to travel to school by bus. it was usually dark when we had to make our way home from the bus. She was particularly worried about the Loughglynn Convent Avenue as the beech trees met overhead like a vast cathedral nave and made an almost impenetrable canopy. The only light was a glimpse of the rising moon as it filtered through the trees and glinted on the lake.

She got in touch with Roscommon Co. Council, and suggested that the avenue should have lights. The request caused a bit of an uproar at Roscommon County Council. At first the leader of the Council assumed that it was the Reverend Mother in Loughglynn who wanted the lights. "What does she want lights for" he spluttered indignantly, "she never lets the nuns put a foot outside the door unless she's with them." Another councillor spotted that it was 'the Ballagh nun' who wanted the avenue lit up for her girls. "Her girls, what girls" growled the leader. "Any road, isn't there lights in the wood all the time, isn't it supposed to be haunted."

The fact was 'the girls' didn't want any lights. The avenue was formerly the road to 'the big house', it was steeped in history. The Demesne wall which surrounded it was built by the Loughglynn dispossessed people in 1800 when the Act of Union was passed. Local people were forbidden to enter inside the gates, now the massive rusting iron gates, symbols of oppression, were thrown carelessly to the side and the avenue was ours. It was magic. We knew every stick and stone and blade of green grass there. The Councillor was right – of course it was haunted. It was full of ghosts – the ghosts of the gentry as they rode in their elegant carriages – the ghosts of the native dispossessed as they keened over their lost heritage – and latterly the ghosts of the young freedom fighters who were immortalised in the ballad *The Woodlands of Loughglynn*. Yes, the avenue was another road that linked us with the road to Ballagh town, and all the generous people and friends that we met on our way, who helped to shape our lives and to prepare us for all the other foreign roads on which we were destined to travel.

> Think where man's glory most begins and ends,
> And say my glory was, I had such friends
> W.B. Yeats

CHAPTER FOURTEEN
THE FIRST TIME
I THOUGHT ABOUT LEAVING

> I watched a mother say farewell
> And all the love that ever filled
> A woman's heart o'erspilled
> And fell in crystal clear misgivings
> On her weary shoes
>
>   Duncan Bain

It was on a bitter cold December morning when I set out with my family from my home in Loughglynn to catch the train to Dublin on the first leg of my journey to London into the unknown. Since then I have a dread of railway stations as I always associate them with the traumatic experience of leaving my home and my family. It was awful painful saying good-bye. The drab waiting room was crowded with young men returning to England after the Christmas break. They were all dressed in navy blue suits and tan shoes which made them look curiously alike, it was a sort of national uniform of the time which probably gave them a sense of security and togetherness. Some of them wore trilbys, but most of them were hatless and carried macks on their arms, their cracked fibre suitcases lay at their feet. All of them were probably in their late teens or early twenties like myself. One young man carried a button accordion; he held it lovingly as if it was a precious baby. They smoked endless cigarettes and talked about their chances of "getting a start" with the big demolition contractors when they arrived in London, Birmingham or Manchester. They talked about lodgings and land-ladies and sleeping four to a bed; they were hoping that the beds wouldn't be too damp after the "holidays". One of their friends caught pneumonia and was very ill as a result of this during the previous session. One lad said he often used the Rowton houses when moving from city to city in search of work; if they were full there was always "Mrs Greenfield" to fall back on. They all laughed at this, but they agreed that sleeping rough was sometimes preferable to the landlady who frequently ripped them off and exploited them unmercifully. You could see they were putting a face on things and that underneath they were wretched, the song was knocked out of them. I was wretched too, and desolate. I wished I was a young man going to work on the demolition sites so that I could share their camaraderie. Girls seemed to be thin on the ground that bitter December morning, with the exception of a group of school girls wearing the uniform of a prestigious convent school in Dublin. They visibly distanced themselves from us.

Vera and family in 1950. In the background, part of the house where Bergin and McDermott left the morning they were shot.

The mothers were mostly huddled together, some of them were fussing around their sons. They all wore drab black coats and hats and had anxious pinched faces, a few of them were quietly sobbing. "Many young men of twenty" were saying goodbye, the best and most enterprising were leaving Ireland to enrich an alien land. Why are the Irish always saying good-bye? I thought of Pearse's poem, "Lord you are hard on mothers, they suffer at their coming and their going". In Ireland they suffer at the double, I thought, because they're always going. The whistle of the train as it pulled in to the station came as a relief, as the waiting only added to the strain of farewells. We all crowded on and waved a final good-bye to our families, losing sight of them completely as the train went round the bend. The train itself was old and dirty, and still operating on peat. The scene at my home town station was repeated at every station until we arrived at Westland Row. There must be no young people left in Ireland, I thought as the carriages became more crowded. Some of the young men began to play Irish music on their flutes and button accordions. They talked about Irish dance halls in London where you could "have the craic", but more importantly where they played traditional Irish music at the intervals. Most of the dance tunes at the time were born on Broadway and London and Irish music and song was literally gasping for breath and had to be "squeezed in" wherever possible. They told me about jobs that I could try for. They said there was great demand for bus-conductresses or "clippies" as they were referred to on the London transport buses. Canteen workers in factory canteens and café waitresses, especially in the Lyons Corner Houses, were also another possibility. This was hopeful news as there was no work available in Ireland. Eventually we arrived at Westland Row, one of the dreariest stations that I have ever set foot in. We were a bedraggled, tired, and dispirited bunch as we headed for the North Wall and the ferries. We were herded into a tin-roofed quayside shed. We were like sardines in a tin and the air was foetid and stale. It seemed like an eternity before we stumbled on board like stock cattle, everyone rushed to the so-called 'saloons' in order to find a seat. The scene was unbelievably stark and desolate. Water dripped on to the deck from some sort of tarpaulin cover and flowed down to the 'saloons'. There was no vestige of comfort in the harsh scene. Some of the young men rushed to the bars. I was very sympathetic – drink at that minute was merely a survival kit. The ferry was late sailing as five hundred head of Irish beef had to be loaded as well as the human cargo. In the third class the stench from the cattle was overpowering. I sat on my suitcase on the deck and cried until I thought my heart would break. The rest of the night was worse as the wind howled and screamed like a demented banshee, hurling suitcases and passengers' belongings across the sloping deck in wild abandon. Nearly all the passengers, including myself, were seasick. Despite the storm, I clung desperately to the deck rail and thought that I was surely going to die. A young Scottish sailor was very amused t my undignified predicament. "I have a cure for sea-sickness", he said, "what will you give me if I tell you?" "Anything, please, please tell me what it is", I said in between humiliating 'gagging'. "You'll never be sick again if you sleep with a sailor", he said. I was too miserable to be either indignant or amused.

Roger McDermott 1950. Hay-making in the woodfield.

The night dragged on and I was never so glad to spy the faint lights of the Gladstone docks. England could be as Protestant and as pagan as she liked but at that minute she represented dry land, and a relief from the raging sea and the slippery vomit on a sloping deck. There was no glamour or romance for the emigrants – we were powerless and penniless. As we moved into the harbour the storm abated somewhat and miraculously my sea-sickness disappeared. I squared my shoulders (as thousands of emigrants before me no doubt had done) and told myself that it was all a huge adventure, I had nothing to lose, and I was blonde and twenty. As I picked up my battered suitcase prior to disembarking, the Scottish sailor winked at me and began to whistle that haunting melody, "Will ye no come back again". I wiped a tear from my eye as the bells of Liverpool rang out across the Mersey to welcome in the new Year. A new year, a new life, a new dream I thought, as I boarded the waiting train that would take me to one of Britain's vast faceless cities where no-one knew my name.

> For we being poor had only our dreams,
> tread softly, lest you tread on our dreams.
> W.B. Yeats

CHAPTER FIFTEEN
THE CALL OF THE WILD SWANS

"The Irish are even a more scattered race than the Jews. They've gone to every land, sailed every sea, scanned every river, and climbed every mountain range." (Sean O'Casey). And yet they always come back. When I return to Loughglynn I feel a deep sense of peace and tranquillity here on the lake shore where this story was inspired by the historic landscape and the people past and present who touched my life. It was here where I experienced very clearly the call of the past, and the past shapes our future in as far as whatever happens began in the past.

As I gaze across the lake I can see the wild swans glide over the water. To me they emphasise the timelessness and mystery of this historic landscape. They or their descendants still build their nests in the bulrushes which they frequented in my youth. I can see the stately church spire dominating the ancient courthouse which was once the hub of Lord Dillon's vast estates. it is easy to picture the bedraggled tenantry wearily trudging there, clutching the hard earned golden sovereigns which had to be paid for rent on 'gale' days. The threat of eviction and destitution always loomed large over the heads of these ancestors of ours. Today the wild birds fly in and out of its once ornate windows, its original glory and the fear which it inspired is forgotten in the mists of time. The remaining round tower is still there, ravaged but unbeaten, held together by the giant ivy which clings to its tottering host. This ancient tower gives us a message of Loughglynn's history in all its chequered phases from time immemorial. Why, I ask, isn't this historic landmark a listed monument?

The wooded island in the centre of the lake was reputedly man-made by Dillon's tenantry at a mere pittance. The earth, stones, soil and shrubs were ferried across in boats, the resultant picturesque wooded island greatly enhanced the view from the mansion. Today it is a haven for the prolific wild life that abound in the lake. The orchard has gone but the stone wall remains. I miss the frothy fragrant blossom as it cascaded over the walls and scattered its petals in the early spring breeze. The walnut trees which lined the orchard wall have gone, as well as the beautiful horse-chestnuts on the lake shore, whose candle like flowers enchanted us as children. Nothing is for ever.

I can see the sandy road that divided the lake from the swallow hole. It was used as a mass walk by the people in the surrounding villages, and was also used as a short-cut to the village itself. I remember very vividly the people from the various villages setting the world to rights on the way to mass. All these rydes and bridle tracks were formerly used by the gentry of the big house as they took their morning carriage drives. One can imagine the elegant ladies relaxing and enjoying the beauty, while their servants held the parasols over their well coiffed heads. Mercifully, nothing is for ever.

So the whole landscape is littered with reminders of the past - the old school, the army barracks (which is now a private residence), the mansion which is still a convent, the ancient courthouse, the leaning round tower, the haunted woodlands, the hungry grass field where supposedly the ghosts of the crying famine children can still be heard, the famine road, and of course Loughglynn's brave heroes immortalised in song and story and enshrined in its proud history. Yes, Loughglynn the one-sided town can rightly boast of an unrivalled historic and colourful past which is evocative of eras that have gone for ever. "And whatever happens began in the past and presses hard on the future." (T.S. Eliot). And we exiles still come back because

> "No artists brush can paint her scenes, nor can a poet's pen, that lovely lake beyond my dreams called beautiful Loughglynn."

SONGS

The Woodlands of Loughglynn

The summer sun was sinking low,
behind the Western Sea,
The lark's loud song was in my ear
but it brought no joy to me,
For the one I loved has gone for e'er
he has left his tyrant's din
He fought 'till death and then he left
the Woodslands of Loughglynn.

He was a noble young Irishman,
John Bergin was his name,
He belonged to Tipperary and from
Nenagh town he came,
But now thank God that he has gone,
he has left his toil and sin
He fought 'till death, and then
he left the Woodlands of Loughglynn.

McDermott too was brave and true,
from the plains of Ballinagare,
He is missed at many a fireside
at home both near and far.
He is missed at home in Tully too,
by his own dear kith, and kin
And he's missed by all his comrade boys
in the Woodlands of Loughglynn.

When our heroes they were dying,
they called for a clergy-man,
Let no one think that they confessed
to an English black-and-tan
The Canon came and was on time
to say the last "Amen" when
McDermott was departing from the
Woodlands of Loughglynn.

John Bergin said that he was proud
to die for an Irish cause,
"The deed was done, that should be done
against England's cruel laws"
Saying goodbye to Tipperary, and to
every vale and glen,
And to all my faithful comrades, in
the Woodlands of Loughglynn.

"Take this message to our own brave
boys, and tell them we are dead,
Tell them to be of utmost cheer, and to
hold no drooping head,
To keep old brains a using, to fight
and not give in,
And be proud to die 'neath an Irish sky
in the Woodlands of Loughglynn.

These were the words our brave boys said
as they died for Ireland's cause
To free our land from black-and-tans
and cruel alien laws,
Goodbye old friends fight side by side,
like gallant Irishmen,
So they closed their eyes, and bade
Good-bye to the Woodlands of
Loughglynn.

Author unknown

Beautiful Loughglynn

There's a picture haunts my memory, I hope to see one day
It's a beautious spot in Erin's Isle, and not so far away
Its lovely valleys decked in green by lake and flowery glen
It's all combined and here to be seen if you visit sweet Loughglynn

And as you go along that road, well shaded in by trees
The fragrance of the sweetest flowers are wafted by the breeze
The thrushes notes are soft and sweet, and linnets sweetly sing
They fill the air with music sweet around my dear Loughglynn

Within the convent's sacred grounds with the holy nuns in prayer
Sure many a day I've spent with you when free from every care
And if I can judge rightly you would have to take a spin
And view the ideal of my dreams in beautiful Loughglynn

Tis there the swan glides gently on, the fish leap to the fly
Its crystal waters bright and clear beneath a cloudless sky
And as the sun sinks in the west it casts its rays again
I fain would stay and take a rest in beautiful Loughglynn

I've seen the River Hudson and the rocky shores of Maine
The beauty of Long Island and Connecticut's fair plain
But oftimes I am lonesome and would love to take a spin
To view the village of my dreams called beautiful Loughglynn

No artist's brush can paint her scenes Nor can a poet's pen
That lovely lake beyond my dreams called beautiful Loughglynn

Miss Greevy (an exile from Lisacul, I think)

The one-sided town of Loughglvnn

Many years since I left dear old Ireland to travel far over the foam
To toil in the land of the stranger, far away from my own native home
Those memories of childhood I cherish, tho' I never may wander again
Round that cave on the hill of Cloonbunny,
Near the one-sided town of Loughglynn

I remember the bright Sunday mornings,
as we gathered around by the cross
As we waited the toll of the hand-bell, twas a signal to enter for mass,
Now that old church has vanished for ever, and I never did wander within,
That new one which now has replaced it, in that one-sided town of Loughglynn

I remember the forge at the corner as we gathered around by the door,
To hear the sledge ring on the anvil as the sparks they bounced over the floor,
Yes, its oft times I blew on that bellows, as the blacksmith did whistle and sing,
As he forged out a loy for the hard working boy
In the one-sided town of Loughglynn.

Now those fifty long years they have vanished, but the memories to me are as plain
Of those days when we went a bird nesting, to the flaggerts around the main drain,
I can hear old McGann with a sweet mellow voice as "the colleen deas" he did sing
The Rose of Tralee or The Banks of the Lee, at a Xmas pig-fair in Loughglynn

But alas what a change has come over the land, when England sent over her villainous band
To torture the aged and to plunder their homes, and to murder the youth of our land

Now those that were babes when I sailed away — Shannon, Carty and
        Glynn —
who fought and who died on that woody hill-side, on the one-sided
        town of Loughglynn

Still the boys of today are as true to the cause
They have sworn that never again
Will the Union Jack fly where those brave boys did die
In the one-sided town of Loughglynn

A Lament for Eddie Duffy

Liberty sits mountain high and slavery has birth
In hovels in the marshes, in the lowest dens on earth
The tyrants of the world pitfall — dig the path between,
And o'ershadow it with scaffolds, prison blocks and guillotine.

The gloomy way is lightened when we walk with those we love,
The heavy load is lightened when we bear and they approve,
The path of life grows darker to me as I journey on
For the loving hearts that travelled it are falling one by one.

The news of death is saddening even in the festive hall,
But when tis heard through prison bars tis the saddest then of all,
Where there's none to share the sorrow in the solitary cell,
In the prison within prison — a blacker hell in hell.

That whisper through the grating has thrilled through all my veins,
'Duffy is dead' a noble soul had slipped the tyrant's chain,
But whatever wounds they gave him in their lying book will show,
How they very kindly treated him, more like a friend than foe.

Still sad and lone was yours Ned, mid the jailors of your race,
With none to press the cold white hand with none to smooth your face,
With none to make the dying wish to homeland friend or brother,
To kindred mind, to promised bride, or to the sorrowing mother.

I tried to get to speak to you before you passed away
As you were dying near to me and far from Castlerea,
But the bible-mongers turned me off when at their office door
I asked last month to see you, now I'll never see you more.

If spirits once released from earth could visit earth again,
You'd come to see me here Ned, but for these we look in vain,
In the dead house you are lying, and I'd wake you if I could,
But they'll wake you in Loughglynn Ned, in that cottage by the wood.

For the mothers' instinct tells her that her dearest one is dead,
That the single mind, the noble soul from earth to Heaven has fled,
As the girls look towards the door and look towards the trees,
To catch that sorrow laden wail that's borne on the breeze.

Thus the path of life grows darker to me, darker day by day,
The stars that shone upon life's path are vanishing away,
Some setting and some shifting, but that one which changes never,
The beacon star of liberty that blazes bright as ever.

O'Donovan Rossa

Mother Erin I have loved thee, with a love that knew no fear,
I have drawn my sword to free thee at the flowering of the year,
But a hand was raised to smite me, as I stopped to kiss thy brow,
And the arm that would have freed thee by my side hangs helpless now

I have lived and loved and laboured with a patriot's heart and will,
That the dawning years might find thee — fearless and unfettered still,
I am vanquished, and my comrades in their glorious fight have fled,
And the loyal hearts that loved thee rest among the silent dead.

They are gone and we must follow to the golden fields above
Where the mighty God of justice shall reward a patriot's love.

Revd. Fr Thompson
(Chaplain to the Franciscan Sisters,1940s,
and buried in the priest's churchyard, Loughglynn)

Ballyhaunis Revisited
Published in the *Western People*

'Tis nigh forty years since I left Ballyhaunis
And cross'd the wild ocean a living to make;
When saying farewell to my friends and companions,
My heart was so sad that I thought it would break.

I remember that morning — 'twas in the gay Springtime
The sun shone out bright and the merry birds sang;
The primrose peep'd shyly from under the hedgerow
While loud in clear air the lone cuckoo's note rang.

'Tho many the years past, it seems but a day since
My father and mother I kiss'd o'er and o'er,
'Twas little I thought when they murmured "God speed you"
My best friends on earth oh I'd never see more.

In the churchyard beyond they are calmly reposing,
Their life's toil is o'er and their spirits at rest;
And often I wonder when thinking about them,
If they ever think of me in the Land of the Blest.

O dear Ballyhaunis, the day that we parted,
A stout strapping gossoon I was, straight and tall,
My hair raven black and my laugh light and hearty
But nobody's left now to know me at all.

I search for old faces, I seek out the old friends
Where where are they gone to – where can they be found?
Ah, some like the swallows have wander'd a far way
And some worn out, have sunk into the ground.

I lean o'er the bridge and I watch the stream flowing,
Its music is soothing and pleasing to hear
I gaze on the hillside and see the old Abbey
Like sentinel looking afar and anear.

Forlorn and lonely I stroll all the streets round
The Main Street and Knox's street, Bridge Street as well,
The Church and the Fair Green, the Square and the Ball Alley,
Each place calls up mem'ries too many to tell.

The saintly old Canon has long gone to glory,
I kneel o'er the spot where now sleeping he lies
A kiss I imprint on the cold ground above him
And pray for his soul with hot tears in my eyes.

I saunter along towards the field where the races
Were held in the old times once fam'd Toonaree
But no trace of the horses the tents or the grand-stand
Nor merry crowds jostling at all can I see.

With ghosts of the past is my memory haunted
And sad recollections comes thronging around
Deserted and empty my heart feels within me
When things lov'd of yore can no longer be found.

The fair and the market, the pattern and races
Were days of delight for the young and the old,
The sport on the fair green and football on Sundays
Oh, thoughts of my boyhood more precious than gold.

I miss Dr Crean and likewise John M. Conry
The "big" and "small" Waldrons and stout Conor Flynn
Tom Caulfield, John Charles and bold Pat McConville
James Greally, Pat Smyth and some more decent men.

John Mac, Thomas Neary and honest James Lyons,
Mick Murphy — "sthrong boord" as we call'd him then
and jolly Thom Glavey, who liv'd down in Knox Street,
With Gallagher's Sermons held up to his chin.

To name all the friends and the kindly old people,
Whose faces and manners I clearly recall
Would take a long day, from the sunrise to sundown
God's blessing be with them, I pray one and all.

The changes are many I see all about me
And strange are the faces I gaze on today
Familiar old names from the signboards have vanish'd
The new pushing old ever out of the way.

O, dear Ballyhaunis, the first time we parted
A fine hardy lad, throth I was to be sure,
I've roughed it some since, and tho' tough was the struggle,
I can hold my head high — I was honest tho' poor.

My locks are now white, and the years weigh upon me
This brow is all wrinkl'd and furrowed with care,
Like a Trojan I've worked in the thick of life's battle
And won what rewards a poor lad could get there.

To no one on earth do I now owe a dollar
For while the sun shone out I tried to make hay,
And this is no brag tho' I say it as shouldn't
A trifle I've sav'd for the dark rainy day.

Farewell Ballyhaunis I now must be going
But maybe God willing some day I'll come back
To glide like a ghost thro' your streets, lanes and alleys
To see how you live and what things you still lack.

My blessing be with you ev'ry night noon and morning
You hold all that's dearest to me upon earth
The dust of my people and home of fond mem'ries
Adieu, Ballyhaunis and the land of my birth.

A Poor Exile
May 1933

Nostalgia

I sat on a moss upholstered stone
And meander back through memory lane
Primroses bright coloured in profusion glad
Lie couched contented 'neath the great oak tree
And a laughing world throbs with exultant joy
Blackbird and thrush chant their endless song
Larks sweet anthems soar in cerulaen skies
The cuckoo's call echoes from distant woods
Pollen stained bees buzz in clover's sweet depths
And a glad, young world inhales the fresh evening breeze
Children's sweet laughter floats on joyous wings
Lowing cows pad to their milking stalls
Farmers bent, heavy stepped, fatigue laden
Wend their way home to fresh brewed tea
And a dazzling sun sinks in a ball of fire-filled glee
But the wings of fancy melt in dismal moist
Wrapped in grey clouds, inky black
A city mantled in brick, mortar stark
And my heart, heavy and suddenly grey,
Longs for the day of pollen stained bees

Sister Laura McDermott
(As published by the National Library of Poetry)

Bibliography

The Cause of Ireland from the United Irishman to Partition, by Liz Curtis. (Beyond the Pale Publications, P.O. Box 337, Belfast, BT9 7BT)

The Irish Civil War (an illustrated history) by Helen Litton, Wolfhound Press.

The Women of 1916 by Ruth Taillon, Wolfhound Press.

The Emergency – Neutral Ireland 1939-45 by Bernard Share, Gill and Macmillan).

Antiquities, Grose.

National Archives, Bishop Street, Dublin 8.